Susan Hawthorne has achieved something [...] is a work that effortlessly blends scholar[...] produce a rich and intoxicating mix. Moving, evocative, dark and humorous, Hawthorne's poetry is a unique dance between Sanskrit and Ancient Greek traditions, haunting the reader with its erotic and melancholic rhythms. A beautiful work.

—Jane Montgomery Griffiths, Greek Theatre and Classics scholar, Senior Lecturer, Theatre and Performance Studies, Monash University; author *Sappho in 9 Fragments*

This 'Cow' has Grade A milk, rich in ideas, wordplay, myth, science, philosophy, humour, sensuality and insight. This is non-homogenised, non-pasteurised poetry, full-bodied and in no need of supplements. To drink these poems is to immerse in a divinely creamy churn of universes, where stars and milk collide. You never know when the next Milky Way will emerge . . .

—berni m janssen, poet, text artist and performer; Asia Pacific Writers Network Project Officer; author *Lake & vale*

Traversing the sentient boundary between human and non-human animals that Western philosophy has worked assiduously to maintain, Hawthorne narrates the local and incommensurable poetics that illuminate the politics of the transnational cow. From dugongs in Indigenous dreaming stories, to the Jersey and Guernsey 'free settlers' and 'migrant' Brahmans, *Cow* moves from Australia to India, via, of course, the moon.

—Keri Glastonbury, Lecturer Creative Writing, University of Newcastle; author *grit salute*

Susan Hawthorne's Cow poems are fascinating, fabulous and ceaselessly engaging. They are intellectually supple and emotionally labile – seductive and demanding, vernacular and subtly formal, sassy, accomplished and compelling reading.

—David Gilbey, Lecturer, Literature and Creative Writing, Charles Sturt University; author *Death and the Motorway*

Susan Hawthorne does a kind of etymological archaeology of Ancient Greek and Sanskrit cultures to recuperate ideas, roles that have been kept secret, suppressed, marginalised and attacked. There are an intriguing number of etymological connections with the word 'cow' and on that level alone, the text is fascinating. Cow is the source, the nourisher, the receptive, but also the secret, the unseen, the rebellious, the creative. She is also sentient, critical, creative, capable, wise and nimble.

—Anna Couani, architect, poet, novelist and teacher of English as a Second Language; author *The Western Horizon*

Taking her lead from 'akam' (Indian Sangam tradition) poems, the collection reflects interiority, heart, household and sexual pleasure. Cows are transposed into myths, or myths into cows (*who says that we should be/the only people on earth without stories*). I will probably never look at a cow the same way again after becoming familiar with how Queenie sees and *tongues* the world.

—Sue Fitchett, poet and clinical psychologist; author *Palaver Lava Queen*

Cow is a real literature that entertains, charms and provokes. Hawthorne's erudition is elegant: she moves from cowshed to cosmos lightly and with technical grace and welcomes you into her fascinating mind.

—Chris Mansell, poet, publisher, literary entrepreneur; author *Spine Lingo: new and selected poems*

Susan Hawthorne is the author of six collections of poetry. Her previous collection, *Earth's Breath* (2009) was shortlisted for the 2010 Judith Wright Poetry Prize. In 2009, she was an Asialink Literature Resident at the University of Madras, India, funded by the Australia Council and Arts Queensland. She is a publisher and Adjunct Professor in the Writing Program at James Cook University in Queensland.

Other books by Susan Hawthorne

poetry

Earth's Breath (2009)
Unsettling the Land (with Suzanne Bellamy, 2008)
The Butterfly Effect (2005)
Bird (1999)
The Language in my Tongue (1993)

fiction

The Falling Woman (2004/1992)

non-fiction

Wild Politics: Feminism, globalisation and bio/diversity (2002)
The Spinifex Quiz Book (1993)

anthologies

HorseDreams (with Jan Fook and Renate Klein, 2004)
Cat Tales (with Jan Fook and Renate Klein, 2003)
September 11, 2001: Feminist perspectives (with Bronwyn Winter, 2002)
Cyberfeminism: Connectivity, critique and creativity (with Renate Klein, 1999)
Car Maintenance, Explosives and Love and other lesbian writings
    (with Cathie Dunsford and Susan Sayer, 1997)
Australia for Women (with Renate Klein, 1994)
Angels of Power (with Renate Klein, 1991)
The Exploding Frangipani (with Cathie Dunsford, 1990)
Moments of Desire (with Jenny Pausacker, 1989)
Difference: Writings by women (1985)

Cow

Susan Hawthorne

SPINIFEX

Published in Australia by Spinifex Press in 2011

Spinifex Press Pty Ltd
504 Queensberry St
North Melbourne, Victoria 3051
Australia
women@spinifexpress.com.au
www.spinifexpress.com.au

© Susan Hawthorne, 1997, 2008, 2009, 2010, 2011

All rights reserved. Without limiting the rights under copyright reserved above, no part of this publication may be reproduced, stored in or introduced into a retrieval system, or transmitted, in any form or by any means (electronic, mechanical, photocopying, recording or otherwise) without prior written permission of both the copyright owner and the above publisher of the book.

Copying for educational purposes
Information in this book may be reproduced in whole or part for study or training purposes, subject to acknowledgement of the source and providing no commercial usage or sale of material occurs. Where copies of part or whole of the book are made under part VB of the Copyright Act, the law requires that prescribed procedures be followed. For information contact the Copyright Agency Limited.

Cover design by Deb Snibson, MAPG
Cover photos by Susan Hawthorne
Typeset by Claire Warren
Printed by McPherson's Printing Group

National Library of Australia Cataloguing-in-Publication entry
Author: Hawthorne, Susan, 1951–
Title: Cow / Susan Hawthorne.
ISBN: 9781876756888 (pbk.)
Notes: Includes bibliographical references.
Dewey Number: A821.3

Title: Cow [electronic resource] / Susan Hawthorne.
ISBN: 9781742195391 (epub)

for Renate

acknowledgements

Some poems in this collection have been previously published (sometimes in different versions) in the following places: *Age, Creatrix, Five Bells, Meanjin, PEN Newsletter, Peril, Sinister Wisdom, Trivia*, the anthologies *Fruit Salad* (1997) and *Prismatics* (2008), and on my blog at http://www.susanscowblog.blogspot.com.

Most of the poems were written while I was an Asialink Literature Resident at the University of Madras, Chennai in 2009. I was funded by the Australia Council and Arts Queensland and I am immensely grateful for their support. Thanks also to the University of Madras for welcoming me to India; to Rajani Pitamber for opening many doors. Special thanks to Eugenie Pinto who gave me a particular poetic welcome and kept on doing so. Enormous thanks are due to Mangai and V. Geetha in Chennai for friendship, stories and poetic support. Each showed me aspects of contemporary life in India that would otherwise have been closed to me. Thanks are due to many individuals for hospitality, meals, music, dance, theatre, conversations and contacts in India. Namaste.

Before, during and after my time in India, I read about Tamil poetry and was influenced by some of its imagery and intrigued by the beauty of the texts (especially A.K. Ramanujan's *Poems of Love and War*, 2008). What I found in these poems was a multivocal approach. The form of the titles – "what she said", "what her friend said" – and so on can be found in Ramanujan's translations. They provide the model for the titles of my poems in *Cow*. In the Tamil Sangam tradition, akam are poems that reflect the concepts of interior, heart, household and sexual pleasure. They are love poems, often written in the voice of a woman. And while it is more usual not to name the characters in akam, my poems draw on a range of other poetic traditions including Greek lyric poetry.

I have been influenced by my language studies in Sanskrit which brought me to Jayadeva's *Gita Govinda*, the *Harivamsha* and the *Ramayana*. I am especially thankful to Greg Bailey at La Trobe University and McComas Taylor at the Australian National University for the different ways in which they have helped me understand the complexities of Sanskrit. I am also indebted to my co-students for their humour and insights; special thanks to Christine Street, Annie McCarthy and Rye Senjen. Via Sanskrit I have returned to reading Ancient Greek and am thankful to Julie Enszer of *Sinister Wisdom* for encouraging me to make my own translations of the poems of Sappho. I have drawn on my earlier readings and translations of the *Homeric Hymns* (to Demeter and Aphrodite) and Plato's *Symposium*, both of which I read as a student of Ancient Greek at the University of Melbourne in the 1980s. The marginalia alongside the poems provide a partial glimpse into my fascination for etymological histories. All errors are mine; some words or lines are intended rewritings. Notes on the main characters can be found at the end of the book.

Thanks to my perceptive readers Kaye Moseley, Suzanne Bellamy, Coleen Clare, Diane Bell and Renate Klein who helped me see the wood for the trees. I am indebted to poet, Jordie Albiston, for her sensitive editing of the manuscript, and to Claire Warren for careful typesetting. Finally, to my partner, Renate Klein and canine friend Freya, for conversations, walks and love.

contents

string three   *what the lovers say*   109

Queenie's loves

In the beginning, the skin of cattle was the skin that humans have now, and the skin of a human was the skin cattle have now.

Jaiminiya-Brahmana (c600 BCE)

etymologies

Cow (kau), sb. [OE. cū = OFris kū, OS. kō (Du. koe), OHG. kuo, chuo (G. kuh), ON. ký́r: Gmc. *kōuz, *kōz, fem., rel. to L. bōs, Gr, βοῦς. The normal descendant of the mutated OE. pl. cȳ (cf. G. kühe) is north. kye; the form kine (now arch.) descends from a ME. (XIII) extension of this with –n from the weak declension, which was mainly due to late OE. gen. pl. cȳna (for cūa).] *Shorter Oxford English Dictionary*

Gau (gavā Gen.) Skrt. cow; anything coming from or belonging to a cow; skin, bow-string; the herds of the sky, stars, rays of light; the sign of Taurus; the moon; a kind of medicinal plant; a singer, a praiser; an organ of sense; a mother; speech; voice, note.

Quean (kwīn). [OE. cwene = OS. cwena (Du. kween barren cow), OHG. quena, quina, ON. kvenna, kvinna (gen. pl., nom. sing. kona), Goth. qino woman: - Gmc. *kwenōn, f. IE. base *gwen- *gwn-, repr. by Gr. γυνή. cf. QUEEN. *Shorter Oxford English Dictionary*

Queen (kwīn), sb. [OE. cwēn = OS. quān, ON. kvæn (also kván), Goth. qēns (wife): - Gmc. *kwǣniz, f. IE. *gwēn-; see QUEAN.] *Shorter Oxford English Dictionary*

string one

the philosophy cow

what the poet says

What we cannot speak about we must pass over
in silence.

Ludwig Wittgenstein
Tractatus Logico-Philosophicus

1

I picture a cow
she is grand and I am small
I walk behind her saying *c'mon*
as low as I can
I shoo her along to the milking yard
    with her calf
I walk beside her rump
and when we reach the wooden gate
she follows me
she knows the routine

I turn to leave
pass by her head her rump
she strikes out with her horns

I will not go near her again
I fear this cow inside me

I have doubled in age and am learning
the internal properties of cow
stand your ground calls my father
as the biggest cow of the herd
breaks away and runs straight at me
I wave my arms about wave the stick at the end of my arm
she is still running
I jump and scream and wave
two metres before I am history
                    she veers sideways and returns to the herd

I have found my cow inside
I have learnt the internal property
that she will give way if you stand your ground
stand your ground I say to myself
even the internal cow is impressed

2

what is a cow?
          an animal
          a symbol
          a statue
          a vocalic
          a smooth surface with all the hair going the same way?

          an economy
          a religion
          a politics
          a mysticism
German: first the cow   an experiment *erst die Kuh dann Du*?
then you.

          a love object
          an orgasm

2

a good meal
a mother
a milkmaid's best and only
friend?
a danger
a lover
a droning sound
a-um
an ocean of milk for all?

a cloud
a constellation
a herd of stars
a word
a voice heard?

the cow is at the limits of my thinking
the native cow
the underwater cow
the marine cow
the unseen cow
the sea-grass eating dugong
a cow in shape and size
a herbivore
what happens to dugong dung?

intersecting worlds
the moment I see the centipede
pulling its hundred legs
over the rim of the wall above my line of sight
ein Blick into another world

ein Blick: German:
a view, look.

the moment when I hear
unspoken histories
genocides

eliminations of the unwanted
every rewriting of history continues that erasure

3

if I assert that xx does not exist
but xx continues
albeit silently and invisibly
who will assert xx's existence?
those who refuse xx
refuse my existence

replace xx with xxy
it is the pseudo-concept
that kills particularity
amoeba-like
surrounds the grain of truth
absorbs
de-differentiates
the name xx is the proper sign
subject
particular

the cow is in the cowshed
sensual cow who sidles up to another
licks her thigh
she is cow both gentle and strong
eats grass but can kill with horns and hooves
she is galactic cow milch cow
origin of all
mother and lover
sister and aunt
friend and cousin

galactic: γαλα,
γαλακτ-: Greek:
milk.

she is the golden calf
worshipped from east and west

Al-Lat Latona Leda
latte bringer
golden calf and graven image
worshipped in the east
worshipped in the west

4

cows came to Australia
with convicts
but there were no emancipations for good behaviour
from five cows have come millions

Indian cows the Zebu from
the colony at Cape Town
like convicts
they escaped went bush
by the time they were found seven years later
their number had increased ten-fold

what happened to these five cows
in the seven years they went missing?
what is the untold story of these runaway cows
these fugitives from empire?

the four-legged cow is not native
but these First Fleet cows
were intent on freeing themselves
from British colonisation

cow culture developed new breeds
the Illawarra official in 1910
gained recognition
visible to the king in England

could they now be killed
milked of their possessions?
migrant cows suffer invisibility
not the Jersey the Guernsey
the Ayrshire or the Holstein Friesian
they are the free settlers
who came to make a living
to improve their lot

I mean the latecomers Brahmans
who live north of the Brisbane line
that line in Australia beyond which
many Australians cannot see

5

if I am a cow what kind of cow am I?
Highlander Jersey Ayrshire
            islanders
Brahman
            east and west combined
what kind of cow is an Australian cow?
            the mermaid cow
            unseen
            endangered
            on the verge of extinction
            her homelands made anew
            into bone-tinkling marinas

did the dugong swim the skies and spill her milk?
did the ocean turn to milk
when the world was tipped upside down
inverted?

are these facts?
are stories about the origins of the universe facts?

are stories about cows facts?
are stories about cows at the origin of the universe facts?

what we cannot speak about we cannot imagine
facts and imagination tangle
a weave of uncertain strings
strings pulled and plucked
edgeless origami in an unfolding universe

6

Io is a white cow a moon cow
the golden calf is a sun cow
the blue cow is a sea cow
the red cow is a menstruating girl
the black cow is the new moon
the starless sky before the cow spills her milky stars

there are cows who do impossible things
the cow who defies gravity
          jumps over the moon
long before rockets
who is to say the moon is not made of cheese left by
          the leaping cow?
there are many conspiracies of silence

there are cows who dance
their four legs beating out the devil's rhythm
cows who make ritual with witches
both untrustworthy beasts in the eyes of religious men

the horned goddess comes to the party
she brings sandwiches and flying ointment
for cows dancing with the moon

Queenie's dilly bag

what she says to her listeners

tales are long and short
they tangle like a chinese noodle in a spiral
a spaghetti in a stretch
a snarl of time
a skein of story

the strings are struck
in exquisite proportion
consonance of lambda
stories told by Chloe and Olivia
by Gertrude and Alice

the planets sing
seven planets seven cows
play rembetika
an uprising of music
seven strings of the baglama

these are stories about cows
who have lost their histories
some say there are no such histories
that they never existed
others say they existed but have been lost

we cows gather on her desk
what is it you want of us?
is it our delightful demeanour
or our marvellous colourful hides?

what Queenie says

queenie queenie who's got the ball?
meanie meanie no one at all

I'm grazing near a human encampment
time has rolled in
on a day the length of all time
I give birth to the folding universe
my milk flows away through the night sky
galaxies spin and twirl form and unform
    as the dance of creation and decreation proceeds

small creatures have come to look at me
they watch the white liquid spill on the ground
it flows like a river forming stars
my calf the size of the earth drinks and grows
stumps and stumbles testing new-found legs
kicks and kicks and the earth wobbles
in that kick she has found power

she is my moon calf
earth calf a fragment of me
her horns only half-grown

Meena: *mīn: Proto-
Dravidian: fish, star.

my calf is called Meena fish
at home on earth
in the sea of sky
where the lunar
ball floats
in the great waters
that flow between creations

what Fatima says about Queenie

Fatima: Arabic: one
who weans an infant,
one who abstains.

Queenie found a place to graze
chanced on it one day as she ate
her way between the stalls
at the vegetable market
she took her time reaching my garden
a poet's paradise at the end of the road
she had thought the market was tasty

when she walked through my open gate
she knew she was home
she'd found a place to return to
whenever she tired of wandering

she'd wandered a lot in her time
ambled over mountains
across deserts
down to the sea
walked through every imaginable farm
spent summers by rivers
once she had visited a friend
in the dark and moist jungle

she had hitched rides
travelled in a cattle truck
her worst experience
she'd pitched about on a boat
had never been on a plane
but that was because of the god-boon
she wished for the power of flight

she'd been to the moon
meandered with taureans
a herd of stars

as bison and boson
Queenie was tired now
she wanted somewhere to cool her heels
to sit back graze away the day
catch up with friends
and talk about the old days

the days of revolution and love
the two coming in and out of focus
daytime it was revolution
night all night it was love

what Queenie says about Meena

I knew from the first kick
before her birth
this one was feisty
they'd have called her bullish
if they didn't know better
Meena suffered no fool not one
on her second day
the day after she wobbled about the garden paradise
Fatima came to my side to milk me
as she'd done since I arrived
but Meena said *no*

out went the hoof and sent the bucket flying
not once not twice but three times
Fatima came once or twice or three times
with the same result
so she gave up on milk curds and ghee
word got out
there was a new challenge in life
to milk Meena's mother

Meena had been kind to Fatima
because I spoke of her as my friend
but when others came Meena was not so kind
the first milker
a lass from down the road famous for her speed
was clipped gently
        thought Meena
on her backside
she fell over and swore
less judicious milkers visited
and Meena let fly

the sound of hurtling buckets crashing
the oomph of a body hitting the ground
the expression of words Meena had never heard

soon Meena was the talk not just of stallholders
but of the entire district
sometimes she lashed out at anyone entering the garden
I said she should tone it down a bit
but Meena said *what for?*
they want my milk I mean your milk that's there for me
and they don't expect me to put up a fight
were they born yesterday?

what the prophet says

she lives in an ancient landscape / myth
and story her daily escape / from a horror
she can't endure / the expectation she'll
be pure / forever an impossible ask / and so
she dons her daily mask / her eyes take in
every muscle / every movement and hustle
in the streets where sewerage sluices
on the corner an old man seduces / time
she stands singing songs / to bring
customers daily she longs / to escape his call
on her to serve / the ragged people for whom
the curve / of her features the shape
of her eyes / is as familiar as her thin disguise
today she's begun the mental tally / of takings
so she can go to the valley / tomorrow
to the place where the wives / gather
with their vessels and their hives / to trace
the path of the old prophet / the one
best known as poet / fifty years ago she'd come
typewriter / in a box and in her mouth the inciter
of rebellion the provider of blankets / and every week
a new pamphlet / they listened they drank her
like liquid / each one on her own became an avid
reader of the shifting alliances / each decided
to take her chances / by escaping this town's
deadly squalor / its impenetrable sadness
and torpor / but then the men rebelled they said
they couldn't get by without their bed / made
their dinner their sex all laid / on and so the women
were made / to stay but for just one day a year
the day of the bees in the valley near / by
they gathered she went intent / on finding
a way to play truant / to disappear in the noise

and clamour / of the day's events she'd use glamour
that old trick she'd read about in books / where
you can see clearly but looks / deceive and
before they know it / you have vanished just like
the poet / who did precisely that on the day
when the men made the women stay

what the mayor says

The cow that strays helps itself to all it gets.

Salma
The Hour Past Midnight

this cow is asking for trouble
bringing disaster upon her own head
if she strays across the paddock
into another world where the grass is green
it's her fault if it's too rich

this cow is a troublemaker
leader of the pack
you can tell from her eyes
the way she looks at you
raising and lowering her head ready to fight

this cow is a wanderer
follows her nose along the tracks
ambles off toward the river
before you know it she'll be bellowing
for rescue from the mud

this cow is untrustworthy
watch how she scrapes her hoof
in the red earth
watch if you will as she stands high
her horns reaching for the sky

a herd of rabble-rousers
and agitators here they come
a social menace
what are we to do
how can we be rid of these firebrands?

what she says to them

who will throw
the first stone?
who will cheer
the stone throwers?

questions that resonate
through the ages

I have stoned
and been stoned
now I despise the throwers
of stones

I will not cheer
for another's demise
it's what
manipulators rely on

followers
unthinkers
those who think
they know better

to stand by
to watch a crucifixion
is to participate
in the crucifixion

hold the stone
raise it throw it
watch the blood come
watch the pain

bury your memory
become like all the rest

will you expect me to rescue
you next month next year
when the stone throwers
come for you?

what Queenie says about Sita

Sita is no slouch just a woman
in the tumult of emotion
she tries to help her man get a life
get out and about
she says *why not follow that deer dear*
she needs time alone
but it's always hard for women
to find solitude
Sita is no different

soon the rival king is coming round
asking for samosas with pickles and chutney
and before she knows it
he has her tucked up in his flying chariot
heading south
she flies with him
to see a bit of the country from the air
but Ravana has other ideas

he tries to woo her
but that isn't why she consorts
a mountain from a molehill
before she knows it the scouts
are arriving on her doorstep
begging her to turn back

why
can't Rama come and ask her himself?
if she isn't important enough
for a visit
why bother?

so she stays on
at the mountain resort
with its beach views elephants peacocks
temples evening dancing
and good intelligent conversation

Ravana too doesn't get it
what is it with these men?
can't they tell the difference
between great conversation and no desire for sex?
(in the case of Ravana)

or great love lust and passion
but no wish to give up on
intellectual pursuits
for housework sitting pretty
and emotional deserts?
(in the case of Rama)

all Sita wants
is a balanced and fulfilling lifestyle
is it really that hard?

she contemplates suicide
this woman who knows her mind
cannot understand why Rama
ten months after her capture
has not come to fight for her
but suicide is hard without implements

and then the war
unwarranted
just as for Helen across the desert lands
there is no end to the bloodshed
the fear the escalating madness
of war hatred destruction

once started
she is no longer relevant to the discussion
she tries negotiating
nothing happening
tries the cold shoulder
only to inflame the passions of Ravana
she retreats
keeps out of sight
one day a great conflagration arises
a river of blood
the palace burns to the ground
Ravana loses his head

Rama stands before her
his eyes cold
his heart stone
there is nothing else for it
but to turn homeward

it hasn't changed a bit
still irrelevant in Rama's list of duties

she sits alone like Penelope
waiting for the man
she thinks she knows to return
before long she notices the early signs
she conceives what is to come
well before her belly swells
this time he evicts her
sends her into exile
she is not much more alone
and here she can
get her life back together
stop waiting for someone to notice her

she starts a school for the study of language
people come from lands all around
they tell stories
recite day-long epic poems
play music
dance and paint
finally life is good
she is revered
among the people
for her intelligence her wit
her sense of justice and fun
they also think her beautiful
one among
many fine attributes

Sita stays in her own country
her children flourish
knowing only a little of their mother's trials

what cows and calves say

thunder bolting at high speed
rolls across the corral
shaking it from root to roof
lightning takes off at even
greater speed and the rain comes
trundling after
                           some calves
are fast like bullets others slow
like cycads watching waiting for
everything to pass them by
high speed or low
                              we speak of memories
of the ways our mothers lived their
lives small udder-sized ambitions
revolving around not losing
what is in your mouth under the straw
or expansive determined sometimes
cruelly controlling
                           the storm
is backing off the resonance vibrating
through our mother's breast a wave
in oscillation we rebellious youngsters
troublemakers unteachable bodytappers
make our own worlds achieving
well beyond what was imagined
Cleis whispers in that teenage tone
look what I've done

what Demeter says to Persephone

next time tell me when you're about to wander off on your own
I knew that bastard had it in for you
munching hyacinths on a hill should be safe
but the world has changed
I heard the pounding of his hooves
but I didn't know he was headed for you

>Ekaterina and Baubo and I
>look everywhere for you
>we climb the hills
>set all the world's eyes alight
>crawl through clouds
>creep into ink dark caves

>no one has seen hide nor hair of you
>days of interminable worry
>no one knows where you are
>I threaten
>I say I'll stop the rain I'll bring cold winds
>no one takes me seriously
>but when the rains don't come
>then they begin to listen

three months it was before Helios owned up
he'd seen that bully taking you down to his yard
why couldn't he have said something sooner?
male ego
>he liked being visible every day
gloried in his own light as if the sun shone out of it

it was the best deal I could manage
so when you're here next spring
we'll take a trip together
a long ramble through the hills
chew the cud and sleep flank to flank

what Persephone says to Demeter

you know I thought I could trust him
but family gatherings are different from solitary walks
when he appeared I was happy to say
g'day uncle
you know how chatty he is
new stories jokes always the funny charmer

so when he said
why don't you come home with me
and have a drink on the terrace
I thought finally someone thinks I'm grown up
well I wasn't ready for the kind of grown-upness
he had in mind

I screamed
but no one in that godforsaken hole could care less
they've seen it too many times
I tried to leave but they barred my way
said since I'd eaten that damned red pomegranate
I had to stay

I was so relieved when you came knocking
so it was auntie Ekaterina who told you where I was?
I'd given her up as a gossip
please tell her again thanks from me
maybe we can visit her
when I get out of here next spring

what Queenie says about trivia

trivia: Latin:
three ways.

three cows meet on a roadside
they sit talk pass on information
Queenie twirls grass in her mouth
making a strand of wicker
she bends a curl
a centrepiece
combines it with others
builds on it
going round in circles
like stories that intertwine
going on forever

one tells a story about a boy
a boy who was always top kid
always travelled with others
but as before
he is challenged by a newcomer
who says he'll meet him in the carpark on Friday night if he's game

      it's not a good week
      it's a week of miseries for our poor Hektor
      his mother is on at him to get a decent haircut
      and does he really need to go to the gym so often
      that his chest becomes like a barrel
      but the gym is irresistible to Hektor
      he's there daily clutching at weights
      turning the chaotic world around him into order

      Friday comes and the newcomer waits under the streetlight
      whistling
      he can hear the beat of piano strings
      strands of jazz from a nearby club
      sounds of rebellion

Hektor arrives alone for the first time
his fingers twitch while he tries to stave off panic
how will he play it
his mind is a carousel
music spinning out through the prancing horses
they size one another up

Queenie stops her story
no point in continuing
it's only ever the lead up that's different
from here on it's either a stalemate
where nothing much happens
or it's a fight to the death
and then we have to listen to the horror
of poor Hektor being dragged
around the carpark by the victor

a silence made of breezes birds and insects
descends over the three cows
the third is humming a tune
an old tune they'd all learnt years ago
but she's the only one who hums or sings on her own
she raises her voice
turns from humming to singing
kine: Middle English: soon all three kine are singing together
cows collectively.   beside the road

30

what Kuvalaya says

rain clouds are gathering at the edge of the world
when we enter the forest the trees
gather their branches over us darken the day
shadow hides us from one another

Sarasvati's speech turns our simple words
into poetry like the mane of a galloping horse

they call me Kuvalaya the night-opening flower
I sing with them carry words
to faraway places to a land across the sea
where once they say
millennia ago
some of their ancestors retreated
others dispute this
and none of the legends is conclusive

I come as a visitor I come with a head full
of words full of landscapes and languages
whether I find my world in the lyrics of their
world is for me to discover here the herd
plays I enter this world of shadows of half-told
stories where the lotus opens at night

what Sita says

I'm straight and I'm deep
I have to be
pulled from the earth as I was
snug in the furrow
earth enfolding me
warm and moist and womblike

I'm the result of a cow and a plough
the cow walks the line of the field
the plough makes the furrow

what neither knew
was that there I lay
wrapped in earth's cloak
feeling the fire sweep across the grass
feeling the rain trickling through
the tickle of earthworms
the magic of mushrooms

history is one thing
you won't find me there
you need to dig for me
you need to burrow
underground
follow the motherlode
the seams of soil and rock
bedrock and magma
burrow until you reach the centre

what she says about shadows

a cow and her shadow
walk a street in Kathmandu

the cow is painted
the shadow is plain

both are black
as the night sky

the shadow says
how come you're so pretty today?

because it's good luck on cow day
so my friend painted mandalas

on my backside says the cow
and what about the garland of flowers

who gave you that?
asks the miffed shadow

the same friend says the cow
feeling sorry for her undecorated friend

tell you what says the cow
you can have the garland now

and at the end of the day
you can have the mandalas too

when the sun goes down
the shadow cow is happy to see

the painted cow has kept her word
there on her shadow back

shine the glittering lights
of Deepavali

what she says about Elektra

at midday the shadows crumple
she is gorging dandelion desire
making daisy chains with her tongue
but the world is full of disloyalty life's debris
destiny's door held ajar a moment too long

this life will wield fate heavily
as hatred stirs her blood
an epic of splintered words shattered hope
exile an unbidden future

the hands of the jeweller are large
her grip on the world strong
but even she cannot hold this little god down
Elektra's stall has been waterproofed
but still the damp creeps in

her curiosity not yet abated
she sniffs at the day in animal thrall
walks thrice round the wheel
before settling down

the kettle-drum rumble of earth
comes and goes in waves of vibration
years of groping at the volcano's throat
rockfall gathering at its base
the yeasted bread of lava bubbling

meanwhile Elektra stands in sadness
yoked to the wheel
just as her mother had demanded
her body pulled tight as rope

the bedrock is crumbling
meaning shattering in a complex
of explosions no one is safe
in this poisonous air filled with
the ash of erupted hope

what she says about Lakshmi and Sarasvati

things are not as they appear
take Sarasvati and Lakshmi
like all good Indian goddesses
they are multi-armed experts
at multi-tasking perhaps even
the originators
                    Lakshmi
the owner of many cows
is good at wealth and fate
she carries a lidded pot
a Pandora's box of sorts
only she knows what is inside
she's dressed in red and rides
a crocodile who will take its
competitors into its mouth
hold tight and roll hoping the
victim will breathe water in fear
you can find Lakshmis in all the
big corporate and government
offices
            Sarasvati is of a friendlier
cast of mind multi-talented
she can speak a host of languages
find her way around foreign
cities entertain with her erudition
and music / only a four-armed
goddess can play the veena like her
only a goddess who knows what's
written beneath the surface
text between the lines could
also sit astride her hawk
and sing sweetly through the
densest philosophical argument

she'll seduce you with her logic
persuade you with her voice
race you to the next theatre
and outdo you in arm wrestling
you'll have to look for her
she's as rare as hens' teeth and
when you find her / smile

what she says about Ereshkigal

a coracle of cattle sailed the black waters
to find the point where the worlds were
      interwelded
from that point a thread was thrown
thunderclouds fell across the void
      uprooted
the known worlds quenching drought-
wrought years drenching dust
      the jester
in the corner was squeezing flesh
removing a splinter from her thumb
      Ereshkigal
changed the world when she picked dirt
from under her fingernail like a
      fletcher
plucking feathers to balance the arrow
shot in memory of the suicidal girl
      abducted
by an uncle on a horse her mother
in endless search for her bringing
      drought
her voice hoarse with wailing her tears
drowning the world in oceanic darkness

what Io says

he came at night
every night he hung around
like a stinking cloud
whispering vileness
I said it clearly
no no no

Hera was on my side
and set the all-seer to guard me
but with some kind of glamour
every single eye
all hundred of them
closed
lulled by cloud lullaby

when the clouds go
you can see me
white as the moon
my horns as sharp
as any virgin's

in my spot under the olive tree
I shimmer like lunar veils
but that temenos that holy place
was plagued
by a cloud of gadflies

no matter how fast I ran
no matter how much dust
this heifer kicked up
no matter where I went
the gadfly stuck to me
sent me mad

until I arrived at the sea
at the crossing now named for me
Bosphoros cow bearer
I swam those black waters
reached the far shore

the fire god calmed me
said *keep on travelling*
one day we'll sing for you
Io with the moon in your eyes

Bosphoros: Greek:
ἡ βοῦς cow; φορος
bearing.

what Hathor says

I'm the universe
my back holds up all the sky
where you can see the great River Nile
flowing each night
my four legs keep stars and earth apart
lest water submerge the earth

I come from the land of seven heavens
walk the desert sands
I travel with bands of young women
carrying tambourines
they wear headdresses in honour of me
the disk and the horns

I'm the flood at every birth
the drought at every death
beyond each gateway is a path
that leads directly to me
if you can't find me
look among the reeds by the river

what Queenie says about Guinevere

Guinevere: Norman
French, form of Welsh
name Gwenhwyfar.
kween: Dutch: barren
cow.

the world is old
and very wide
my cousin Guinevere
tells me so

old Gwen new bride
her face like a cloud
a snow-dressed mountain
a spill of milk

the cattle rustlers
are busy in her land
where the edge of the world
falls into the sea

here wander fairy cows
abandoning the dowry
farmer-reined
their gifts fattening

but good luck turns
to greed and when he
raises the knife
the bridle magic ends

come yellow cow
stray no more
enter the lake
come home come home

and so the fairy cows
return to the waters
each one marked
by a waterlily

what Durga says

it's a human struggle
the rising of the soul
but in this rising are
a host of players

my lion will eat your
lamb for Sunday lunch
but I'm as sweet as Mary
swathed in her blue gown

I'm a Disco Durga
a multimedia event
sharper and louder
than the local girls

I like the theatre life
its procenium arches
pantomimes and processions
drumming beats my heart

I'm not a morning person
not for me early morning chores
raising the sun milking kine
rounding up life

give me the limelight
the starlight the darkness
give me the narrow alleyways
where I can strangle silently

or give me an audience
and I'll do my gomukha
a haka my livid face
will scare you from your seat

gomukha: Sanskrit:
cow-face; also a
position in yoga.

43

the accusations have been bold
murder betrayal resistance
protection rackets
blood and bitterness

but that is just publicity
they don't like my mouth
spitting bloodied torsos
in the words I speak

they say I killed Crime Boss
Number One cleaved his head
like an unwanted weed
leaving limbs not scars

they don't like my friends
my lion my tiger
my seven-headed cobra
but I too am lotus-eyed

give me the quiet
of gin-and-tonic evenings
and I'll tell you a thing or two
I'm really very likeable

your soul is safe with me
safer than with anyone
for I can make your soul
rise as high as the sky

what she says about Kalypso's secret

Kalypso:
καλυψω: Greek:
cover or conceal.

our histories are told in entrails
in case they find a stain
we have a shadowless history
rarely fall from the onlookers' eyes
our limbs loose as anything
we are nowhere to be seen
will a glance from another world
doorway like ancient Kalypso
my city was nothing but a hole
you had to crawl through
beware the meshings of webs
a vibrating violin string
braces you for the future

no one wants to look
to make the sanest of us fret
one in which the scales
we take refuge in loving
our loves even more complex
questions so rarely asked
take us through that hidden
concealed among the cypresses
burdened by loam and rock
squat when you arrived
slung low across openings
that makes you hum
a future that never comes

what Savitri says

I know the secret
of how a world can shift
I use every trick in the
book outdo them all
by my devotions I am
an ancient Simone
Weil giant of piety
I know my mind
I will action through
interiority

I'm a pilgrim going
to the forest that great
cornucopia of asceticism
I out-abnegate kings
and gods I overcome
their authority
even Yama
powerhouse
of death

I am defiance and
obedience wrapped in a
single cloak
my will my speech my actions
shout compliance
my will my speech my actions
whisper disobedience

what she says about the wilful virgin

the 105-year-old virgin says
sex wasn't worth the hassle
this is a simpler philosophy than renunciation of the body's chaos
the idea that the body is always teetering
at the edge of a cliff
trembling
the hair on the back of the neck bristling
like a trigger

time may have grown old along with this old cow
but she is not of the school of disorder requiring salvation
no she is simply too busy to bother with the mess
the rituals
and the scraps of freedom found in the kitchen sink

this one cunning as a wolf
has seen the world
with her countless eyes
not fooled by omens and promises
not one to be annihilated or outpaced
this old tortoise has seen it all
free of delusion
her unwithered body endures
her life an epic in more chapters than most imagine possible
what she conjured at age twelve was no inexorable destiny
but a fate to be resisted
no marriage
no children
no distraction from her wolf-bellied freedom

she has discarded heaven and found a free side entrance
just around the corner out of sight
avoid the tumult

rejoice in the spring of limbs
she refuses corruption
not for purity or false gods
but just to be herself

what the mythmakers say

Queenie is afflicted with post-prandial drowsiness
her four stomachs all churning together
Queenie is no fool she's been around for a while
since the beginning of time
who spilt the milky star road?
who set the galaxies spinning?

it's Queenie who taught us how to make butter and ghee
                    the churn
her own invention
            take one stomach
            fill with milk
            stir with a wooden stick until the cream separates
            move to stomach number two
            turn churn spin and stir
            watch it clump and cluster
            look a little longer until the buttermilk seeps out
            in the third stomach knead and knuckle
            make it smooth and firm
            the fourth stomach will heat the butter
            and turn it to ghee

in another time
a later time
when gods and demons
had forgotten how to be immortal
they joined forces to create a nectar of immortality
these boys took their time
they carried in Mount Mandara
turned it upside down
placed it upon the back of the tortoise
demons one side
gods the other

each held the world snake
twirled the mountain top for a thousand years
back forwards
back forwards
again and again and again
the best they could manage was deadly poison

in the great south land
a snake laps up the cow's spilt milk
this one swallows all the girls and women
swallows the bleeding girls
the pregnant women
swallows them and makes them dance
their insides begin to churn
no one can hold anything down
they vomit they bleed
they are swallowed yet again
by the snake who suffers from indigestion
the girls and women
beat their fists against the stomach walls

when the next full moon comes round the world snake
regurgitates the tribe of women

in a garden between two great rivers
a woman encounters a snake
she is impressed by the colour of its scales   green
she prods it with a stick
and the snake turns blue in rage
the snake is wily
knows better than to broadcast its thoughts
pulling its head in
the snake offers her fruit from the tree
this woman is nothing but naïve

she takes it
bites it with her giant teeth
scraping them along its flesh
she's not impressed with the sour fruit
tosses it over her shoulder

                               walks away

what Queenie says about the sun cow

the sun cow took a holiday
to stay with her sister-in-law
in the mountains
there in the deepest caves
beside the River Rasa
she slept
she slept because she had worked
for too long
for too many
she slept because she was tired of being
at the beck and call of everyone
from toddler to grandparent
and all the old aunties
and various hangers-on

she went to stay in the mountains
because the cave was herself
that dark interior
unexplored
in the cracks of time

(and then he had to spoil it all
accused her sister-in-law
of being demonic
selfish
of abducting the sun cow
and leaving the earth
those poor helpless ones in darkness
he bribed Sarama
the house dog
with promises of all she could eat
and sent her on a grand search)

she sniffed and tracked
and swam raging rivers
in search of the sun cow
found her scent
on the bank of the Rasa
following her nose
she came to her side
nudged her flank and said
he wants you to come home

the sun cow said *stay sister*
this quiet place is heaven
no one to demand another drink of milk
no one to make you carry all the shopping home
no one to insist you raise the sun and bear the world
all day every day
but Sarama had orders to return

(he blusters about those demons stealing
his sun cow
his world
his light
beats Sarama
who quivers and wishes she had stayed
he forces her to show him the way
he can't contain himself
kills his sister and her demon friends
abducts the sun cow
who is flaring and kicking and goring him
between the ribs)

the river still flows
the old caves are empty
the sun cow is at her daily work
holding things together

what Cow and Tiger say

a cow and a tiger — how should they meet in a poem?
logic demands that carnivore — eat herbivore
unsurprisingly — Cow has a better idea
let's have a conversation — says Cow
you sit there and I'll sit here — *and we will talk*
but says Tiger — *before talk I must eat*
no way — says Cow
every civilised being knows — *talking and eating go together*
Tiger takes action — leaps for the throat
no eat no talk says Tiger — mouth full of flesh

what Queenie says about Mahādevī

Mahādevī: Sanskrit:
great goddess.

Mahadevi elephant mother smelt
another being on earth
she says to her friends
it's time for us to walk the world
and so they set off with Mahadevi
in the lead across
the African veld
                 they navigate
seas to the hot lands
spread out through
tundras in the north
cross land bridges and
waterways an isthmus or two
snow capped mountains
                 sometimes they carry
thick fur on their backs which they
shed in the desert lands
eons go by as they walk
seven times around die Welt

die Welt: German:
the world.

                 Mahadevi says
it's here where we started
now I know the common smell
those small four-limbed creatures
whom we've passed in the latest
circumambulation the hairless ones
there is something about them
that worries me
                 as she says this
a group of these small four-limbed creatures
climb over the hill and stare
                 mothers daughters aunties
form a circle around
the calves and send

out a low call to others
that rumbles seven times
                around the world

what Queenie says about the Catalogue of Cows

our earliest epic
is fragmentary
more parts lost than found

sing now of the tribe of cows sweet-voiced singers
daughters of she who brings all stars into existence

this is how it begins

the poet says we roamed arcadia
spread out over the hills
and across the plains
wherever feed was plentiful
we travelled with our daughters
close by our side
the bullocks we sent off after a time
their existence more solitary

some say in that time we were immortal
it doesn't matter since cow and calf are so close
it is as though we are still immortal
and who knows what those old poets meant
when they spoke such words

we are recorded as grass feeders
accompanied by winged harpies
who journeying around the earth
brought others to us
who became known as milk feeders

we were oracles
our pronouncements not to be messed with
our names were listed

Nicothoe Aellopus Ocypete
Harpys and Ocypus
Propontis Echinades Strophades
we were the turning ones
you can see it in our tracks across the land

we travelled by boat
through the islands of the Aegean
and the Ionian seas
our boats were winged
they cut through the seas like curved knives

from time to time we saw the blue-faced
daughters of the ocean spring up between waves
now and then they brought gifts
we watched as Helen sped off with her lover
and we wept when poor Iphigeneia
was sacrificed
but it was not our doing
even then they distorted the stories

our longest journey was eastward
we were so numerous the dust clouds
could be seen from the sea
we wandered those wide paths
encountered every kind of strife
were tangled in thorny bushes
and found ourselves in great swathes of trees
giant-legged beings

we did not know where we were headed
only that war threatened our existence
and so we plodded on through mountains
and valleys until we reached the great River Indus
where we stayed

we strolled about the green pastures
the people there were peaceful
they welcomed us
they worshipped us
here we were safe

string two

what the philosophers say

Diotima

how the words on the page
are to be read
measured
understood

that old bull Socrates calls an afternoon
meeting a gnosh up
of food and talk
all about love

they go around the circle
each one
in the steers' stall
taking his turn
to speak at length

Socrates can't stop talking
about the concept of fecundity
at the heart of my philosophy

since the bull walks off
how can we expect
him to invent a theory
of existence founded
on the metaphor of pregnancy?

I'm no figment
of his imagination
too real to conceive
through solitary thrills

becoming he calls it
a dynamic philosophy
concocted over my kitchen table
a trapeza
two equilateral triangles

trapeza: ή τραπεζα:
Greek: table; also a
rectangle comprised of
two triangles of ten
dots.

how the dots on the page
are to be read
measured
understood

a stack of wood
intervals
the lambda letter
from the snake's mouth

when I'm in full flight my intellect
swings I explore
not static existence
but moments of between-ness
the metaxu

metaxu: μεταξυ: Greek:
between.

the amphibious zone
between existence
and reality a method
of communication

the wall at the dead end
the means
by which prisoners
speak

Gargi

how words are heard
a great listener I am
I have to be
because my words
are not welcome

my name is Rishini Gargi
I am plain precocious
a composer of hymns
daughter of a sage

ṛṣṇī: Sanskrit:
female sage.

I challenge Yajnavalka
who claims that *being*
cannot be named

a word weaver
stringing him along
I ask
on what is the world woven
warp and woof?

he demeans me
don't think too hard
girlie
your head will burst

haven't we all heard
that thinking
will make you unattractive?

and so I persist
I keep on asking questions
he has an answer
for everything

not impressed
I accuse him
of being incapable of listening
incapable of thinking
I think *why bother?*
stand up and leave

walk through the between
space flanked by impermanence
the matrix the otaprota
the woof and warp of existence
reality stitched
the universe
a sound strung
string bag
dilly bag

otaprota: Sanskrit:
sewn lengthwise and
crosswise; matrix.

on the other side
sanatana
the old eternal philosophy
the unchanging nature of immortals
the wall which divides
these prisoners

sanātana: Sanskrit:
unending, eternal.

how history is passed down
not vertically
but by twists and turns
a knot in the
labyrinth of lies and dead ends

Queenie's tongue

what she says about ruminants

a ruminant has four stomachs
like the four directions four winds

the rumen is for thinking
chew it over
separate the layers   liquid from solid
create the bolus that rises
not once
but repeatedly   coming and going
regurgitate meditate
the cud thoroughly chewed
until it is thoughtfully digested

rumen: Latin: throat, gullet.

the reticulum is the dilly bag of the system
honeycombed
a latticed fishing net
the cow carries about her grazings
sifting and sieving
her colander
a net covers the mouth
between
stomachs like a doily on a milk jug
the intestine's caul

reticulum: Latin: small net; a small constellation in the summer sky.

this cow is reading with her stomach
it hungers it turns it squelches
the leaves of the omasum flip
like the folios of a book breathing
this stomach folds around time
meditates and reflects
her pages scored with acid
etched memory of enzymes
        finding passage
through the wall like ghosts

omasum: abomasum: Latin: stomach; leaf; folio.

67

the abomasum can stomach anything
the second book its contents
digested in all the usual ways
of monogastrics
here I tell you what
I have hungered for

what she says about the anatomy of a cow pat

where they drop and when
is all important
consider this

on the savannahs of Africa
and in the deserts too
a special follower evolves

the dung beetle
        watch the little body
        work like a Trojan to roll
                that corner of
                that dung heap across
                that road
                        like Sisyphus
                        or ordinary housework
                        this is an endless task

in tropical regions
India northern Australia
        temperature
        humidity
        and battalions of insects
        ensure the dung
        dissolves in days
                to make use of it for fuel
                she must be quick
                follow the cow
                        pick it up
                        dry it out

on the dry plains
of the western slopes
where the nature of
soil and brick merge
    the cow pat sits
    and sits
        waiting for the children
        to walk past
            they pick them up
            toss them like Frisbees
            watch the universe spin

what she says about tongues

these words are worn
utterable like the tongues of poems
there are no confessions
we make our own gilt
paranoia is hermetic
sealed as only a mind can be
unutterable like the tongues of poets

śūnyatā: Sanskrit:
emptiness; drawn from
śunya: empty; void.

what Queenie says about shunyata

the new moon is a black void in the night sky
but it is still there
the full moon is a zero
nothing overlaying something
the zero of emptiness
a bounded hollow is it a void?
how many zeros can a woman sew?
who swells the devil's eye?
every cipher has its codebreaker
and it's Eros who breaks
the code of longing
the lover's absence
the hollow feeling in the chest
the zero feeling of loneliness
hanging by
an unstranded rope
in the emptiness of
shunyata
the missing person begets
herself just like
a parthenogenetic cow
begotten in terra nullius
of unknown parentage
the fall into desolation
when she is seized
bathetic gloom
her limbs loosed
far too much
unshackled
she trips and darkness
like a pack of unruly dogs hounds her
the moon does its rounds a zero
without a binary

what the fool's lover says

the fool begins with zero
0
the vanishing point
the body
standing in the gap
with no
thing in the middle

she stares into
absence
the place that is
void
she asks *is it*
empty?

I answer *no but it is*
silent
we do not live to experience
death says
Wittgenstein

are we there yet?
asks seven-year-old
Xena in the back seat
will we ever
be there? she persists following
Zeno's lead
can we see it?

we shall
be it says Wittig
we shall be
the body not standing in

the gap
not existing in the
lacuna not the stranger

we shall
begin again at
0

what she says about her girlfriend's mother

one day she looks down the throat of her child
who has been playing in the mud eating dirt
there inside the mouth is the universe
trees seas mountains and everything in between
there are cows feeding calves the milk
spilling around the calves' mouths
a giant snake curls around a tree trunk
the snake and the cow are morphing
the dividing line between them blurred
as the sea's edge on any beach
the mothers are trying hard to contain their children
but what can you do when the world is held
in an open mouth?

ur: German:
original, ancient.
ūrochse: Middle High
German: European
bison, aurochs: Old
English oxa: ox.

what her mother says about ur-woman

her face is a mirage
a reflection of who we are
as she teeters on the edge
of the visible like a reflection
in a lake appearing disappearing

we know her as the moon's calf
a fragment a word here a word there
her story gone from the annals of history
missing from the genealogies
she is an absence a plain white sheet

she is ur-woman elemental
floating in a cloud of song
leaping from cliff into flight
she is in exile from time
her realm the inner eye

she is one of the missing persons
we look for her in old manuscripts
among the gopi dancing in forests
she is shameless and in love
her actions of passion unconstrained

gopī: Sanskrit:
cowherding women
who live in the forest.

she leaves home for exile
stands her ground against those
who would poison her
with words or tinctures ˙
and then vanishes

what Queenie notices about dictionaries

as always the dictionary has
a gap a space a hole a lacuna
a string of woven hair

the lexicon a spin of thread
a crack a fissure a perforation
a tear a breach a slit a pause

a love porous and calf-like

what the linguist says

I dig for language as if tilling
will raise the dead
I dig down to bedrock
so hard that my hooves crack
it doesn't open the language
through the middle as hoped

I dig for language turning topsoil
earthworms make scripts
underground three dimensional
tunnels of language
I dig hard
plunge my horns into rock

I dig for language uprooting words
from the trail of historical
syntax across continents
down through tap roots
the shapes of letters and words
frizzing on the edge of a root

well down past the roots
on the other side of bedrock
into earth's magma I find
this earth inside me like ice
filled with a silence I can't navigate
I have dug right through language

what the linguist says about Queenie

she was dancing over India
and out fell the languages
thousands of them written
in hundreds of alphabets

a dancer and linguist
Queenie steps out the letters
in the sands of Phoenicia
aleph alpha alif ox and cow
travelling east and west
her hooves have split
the letters morph through
Tocharian and Gandhari
Prakrit Sanskrit Tamil and Pali

āleph: Hebrew aleph,
Greek alpha, Latin a,
and Arabic alif are
descended from
Phoenician āleph, from
a reconstructed Proto-
Canaanite alp: ox.

there are many trade routes
many tales in the passage
of these letters finding the
edge of sound and shape
she traces vowels in the cave
of her mouth the consonants
travel from larynx to lips

she teaches them the sound of the universe

she collects alphabets
vowels pitch in her mouth
stopped with consonantal flourish

the first word she remembers
learning to read in this life is *idea*

oh the contour of that word
three syllables packed into four letters
just the dental in the middle

she was dancing over India
chasing an idea
chasing a history
in some languages
yet unmade

what Queenie says about pedagogy

my specialities are ancient
they say I am dead
and my languages too but you can't ignore
my methods

my body informs me
my students numerous
from the cow comes a method of learning
four-footed and sure

first foot is the teacher the knower the one who
inspires you to take that stretch parse
that sentence finish that translation understand
that construction

second foot is the student the driven one who
spends all afternoon finding the right ya out of
forty-seven uses drives her girlfriends crazy
with complexity

third foot is crowded with students
the one who sings on the beach untangles
a phrase with elegant simplicity understands
your linguistic clumsiness

fourth foot is the most uncertain
dragging foot fast-paced foot always behind
forever ahead there is never enough
for time cannot be confined

what Queenie says about Tamil

how the letters land
might be an indicator

in Tamil
the letter on all the temples

is the same sound
aum om

in Tamil
it resembles

ௐ : Tamil: om.

a giant ear
at the centre of the universe

listening
listening

to the music

what Queenie says about Sanskrit

language is perpendicular
roots elude her
gerunds are thick with meaning
she slips falls
crashing to the ground

> where they drop and when
> is all important
> in the cow circus

she climbs a conjugation
declines a declension
all the while the endings tangling

> we do on four feet
> what you can barely imagine
> on two

seven mountains crossed
each one higher than the last
participles present not too much challenge
the passive is aggressive

consider the six-high rump stand
> head
>> tail
> head
>> tail
> head
>> tail

she has etymological epiphanies
blinding insight
finds it is the wrong form
the wrong verb
an unknown Vedic version

on trapeze
   hoof-hang
   udder hang
the former quite easy
the latter some discomfort
but pain they say
is to be overcome
I say *avoid it*

she has taken to reading
the dictionary
forwards backwards
horizontally
vertically

   my favourite is the web
   rise up in a Russian climb
   hook in a hoof
   tuck and wait for the spin
   wait until the speed is high
            then   s p l a y   o u t
   three legs flying
   one tail whipping the air

sandhi: Sanskrit:
junction.

sandhi
internal and external
takes her on
another spin
down the rock wall
falling is easy
she hopes she never lands

   spin at the end
   like a stellar top
   the star Aldebaran
   red Rohini
   follow the sisters

84

in their flight
think yourself light
as helium float
your way to the top
up here I can feel the universe spin

what she says about language

she was drowning
not waving in the
rip of language
help she called
breathless
the cold of its logic
wrapping itself about
her limbs
             swim across
the rip through the
decline let the wave
and its rhythm carry
you in when you are
ready you will stand
upon your own four
feet don't stumble
into the deeps of other
tenses keep a cool
head
             her hooves are
falling out from under
her linguistic dizziness
has her in its thrall
one step two step
three step four step
one breath next breath
next breath next breath
she has found the
shoreline continental
shelf of language her
feet solid on the
             sand at last

what Queenie says about subhashitani

subhāṣita: Sanskrit
equivalent of a proverb;
plural subhāṣitāni.

the elephants   only elephants   are drinking tea
they balance teacup and saucer daintily at the end
of their trunks they are speaking in Sanskrit

the dogs are getting in on the act running in circles
and challenging one another to verbal duels
the numbers in the course crash

the lions are smuggling alcohol into their rooms
secreting it under their beds and turning up drunk to class
where they must sing five subhashitani by heart

the fish are completely out of control they have consumed
many tonnes of tigers who were carrying the poet
their piranha teeth are dripping blood their bellies aching

from the corner of the class come voices
poikilophron these butterflies the rainbow
rages in jealousy ready to draw the bow

poikilophrōn:
ποικιλοφρων:
Greek: many hued,
multi-coloured mind.

the cows are gambling away their futures
they say passion is more important than profit
they sing and chant their hidden histories

the creatures share grammatical tricks and mnemonic
methods they pack up their books their paradigms
their songbooks and fall into exhausted sleep

what she says to her girlfriend

who is this spluttering one
speaking gibberish to a stone?
she utters prayers

as if they were knives
sharpened on a brittle mind
it's the silence that is killing her

she is quietly crying
so passersby will not see the tears
hear the splutterings from her lips

will they ever decode her utterances
fill the gaps
open the world wide?

what she says about gaur

immoveable
ancient as diamonds
old as song
gaur are statues against green

mountains
ridge their backs
verbs crest the ends
of sentences

heads
a saddle between
where water gathers in the wet

the female line
zigzags
the sloped hillside
the dual feminine

Matagavam
mother of the gaur
stands like a giant fortress
at the base
inverting the mountain
top

matagavām: Sanskrit:
cow mother.

early risers
greet the day
moaning low

at night
a multitude
of sickle moons
graze

long-sighted eyes
horns almost a circle
pale summer grass
coloured

rufous coats shining
beneath a harvest moon

what she says about boanthropy

if you stand in the path of a boanthrope
you are bound to get hurt
they are said to be dangerously
out of their minds

imagined horns are razor sharp
keen-edged and infinite
and the boanthrope
is convinced her horns are real

were-wolves and were-cows are travellers
whose appetites are great
bedeck them in garlands
and they will follow you

boanthropy: ἡ βοῦς:
Greek: cow;
anthrōpi: the fem. of
ἀνθρωπος, ἡ, Greek:
(like *homo* fem. in Lat.)
a woman.

91

what nonsense Queenie says about Ushas

seven cows came out of the river
heaven born and heaven sent
cows headed into storm
unafraid of anyone's wrath
the next river is their camp

the wild storm passed they
ate breakfast of raindrop grass
conjured up a golden calf
to carry all their wealth
seven cows went into the river

seven cows came out of the sky
seven hymns to sun's dawn
chariot's gleam of blinding light
waking into cloud-strewn day
seven cows flew away

what Queenie wishes

the wingless ones are here
moving around the mounds
their mouths wailing in grief
wingless widows white as snow

on the other side of the river
sits the wish-fulfilling cow
her gaze complex as chaos
fragile as a fractal

what you say to me

the muscles on your flanks
ripple like quicksilver
the play of your mouth is a die
thrown six times
it flips into the endless sky
a mirror of your soul
you say you want discipline
you want to play
between the lines
of the strictest form
instead you dance in circles
an ancient acolyte
a mystery of Eleusinian proportion
if you tell you die

half way through / you change your mind
walk straight ahead / follow an invisible line of sight

in front of you
nothingness
behind
the land unfolds into existence
at each step
when your hoof touches the ground
it grows reaches out
and away from your red painted hooves
ringing with the sound
of your ankle bells
you are that old gesture
the one only initiates know
you are a mandala
in endless circling motion

what she says to you

your poems are like temples
elaborate and multi-hued
run your tongue over their surfaces
feel the sculptural complexity
hear the ornamented words
thrill to their sounds
their peaks and troughs
soaring pitch and indigo roar
watch as they plunge
like a body falling full throttle
into a bubbling pool of water
like a temple gopuram
your poem is a spectacle
your worshippers circle as they listen
circle toward an unknown
centre of intensity
words packed like Hindu gods
dancing and trembling with delight
in the swirl of your eyes

puram: Tamil, Pali, Sanskrit: tall structure, village, fort, capital. go: from the root for cow (sometimes written ko).

95

what if this is god

she said
the heifer of a girl standing next to me
do you want to see god?
it seemed like too good an opportunity to miss
god available to see

darshan: Sanskrit: seeing.

is this a darshan?
does god see me too?

we walk through the heavy black columns
a forest of elephant legs
pass an old ox walking in circles around one column
has god already spoken to him?
enjoined him to do this?
in penance?
for blessings?

she beckons me to follow
we enter a small alcove
beaten gold walls
a priest inside
he wafts a flame
stows a garland around
is it god's shoulders?
places fruit in a shallow bowl
scoops water for the devotees

tulasi: Tamil: the herb basil, considered holy.

follows it with a spray of tulasi

we leave for another grander alcove
god here is bigger
seems to have company
but again
a flame

a garland of flowers
fruit
a gift of water in a shallow hand
tulasi

I am satisfied
if this is god

what the pedant says

I am a between one / a one and an other
whoever knows me truly knows my world
its shapes its stories its coded memories
I am a between one / a one and an other
amphibious I crawl on sand and sea alike
my fins awash with poems and songs
I am a between one / a one and an other
whoever knows me truly knows my world

amphibious I crawl on sand and sea alike
the passage between realms is slippery
my meanings are so badly translated
amphibious I crawl on sand and sea alike
syntax looks easy from a distance
not reading the spaces between the lines
amphibious I crawl on sand and sea alike
the passage between realms is slippery

syntax looks easy from a distance
the pedant is into semantics all hers
nothing becomes a more than something
syntax looks easy from a distance
something is always more than nothing
and the tricks of no one visible in the hole
syntax looks easy from a distance
the pedant is into semantics all hers

something is always more than nothing
how love fills the void to its brim
its fall is the beginning of its rise
something is always more than nothing
when you are a between / a one and another
saying cruel words with your eyes
something is always more than nothing
how love fills the void to its brim

what we say about exile

there was a time when we were not exiles
a time when paradise was not some imagined garden
walled from our world
paradise was here and now

in that time and in that place
we long-horned four-footed ones
were honoured and rejected
just as often or rarely as anyone

our horns our feet our udders
were nothing special
but they were us

one day someone said
you lot
we looked around to see if we were that lot
yes said this someone
you long-horned four-footed ones with dugs   dugs: related to
it is time for you to go   Sanskrit dugdha:
take with you your golden calves   milked.
for you are no longer welcome here

that was the day we were cast out exiled
from the place some now call paradise
the walls were high covered by thorns

in spite of our usefulness
we were no longer welcome
we were spat upon
great gobs of spit spewed our way
landing if we were lucky at our feet
and if not in our hides and on our skin

99

they sent the children out
from the garden behind the wall
to throw stones at us
you could see them looking
with shining eyes
for the biggest missile
stones and rocks flung by young fingers

we tried to ignore it
walking on in silence
we lowed together
we tried to stop it
but one day one of us
in a fever of anger
lashed out gored him
son of the most
important man
in the village

after that it was all out war
if we ventured through their village
took a short cut across their fields
if they saw our outline on the ridge
they came for us

some of us were killed
some of us were captured

they tied us to the millstone
to the water wheel
had us walking an eternity of circles
yoked us to the cart
whipped us
took us to their battlefields
we hauled we carried we bled
we were abandoned when they fled

some of us escaped
travelled in groups
some toward the rising sun
some toward the setting sun

you will find us in these places
at the edges of every known world
like it or not we are everywhere

what Sarasvathi says

we are slaves to their needs

I am standing in the field
and she says
                    these animals
then you appear and I see my life
in a different shape
I learn that I am not a heap of dung
that my place in life
is not cast as beast of burden
that I too might spend an afternoon
sniffing daisies and clover
as their poets would have it

I ask you to the celebration
and you come
even though the invitation
is in a language you don't understand
you walk through the dark narrow streets
ask your way

my daughter stands in the side stall
her tail a weave of flowers
marigold rose and jasmine
you stand next to her
admire her flanks
nuzzle close

I cease the circling walk
slavish obedience
to the millstone
I resolve to escape
the daily drudgery

what we say about loss

Standen wir nicht / unter *einem* Passat?

Paul Celan

Sprachgitter

German: Were we not standing / under *one* trade wind?
Sprachgitter: German: language mesh.

rain overnight
        and this morning

standing under a single
        great wind

we search for just the right word
        to call our loss

to have our losses seen
        but who will see

who can see
        the fallen ones

unsalvaged from the ruins
        of history's leavings?

that's what she says happened
        itihasa

itihasa: Sanskrit: what was said; history.

and if that's what we say
        who is to judge us?

what Queenie says about the question of language

no one understands anyone else's code any more
the metaphors have lost their power
intensity is all virtual
displaced into ether
language is under a temporary protection visa
disembodied
the life wrung out of it

language boats cast off across oceans
most drown most disappear
without trace under bellying waves   ·
sunk into oblivion
a few refugee codes make the crossing
but in crossing they lose too much
lose their souls
the price of crossing high

our language an untranslatable cipher
has dissipated disconnected
words strewn across pages
disordered rumpled like the skirt
of a woman in a field she's never seen before
like garbage in a disused car yard

the poets are grumbling
they no longer know how to gather the traces
follow the tracks across the trackless ocean
can no longer find the wheelmarks in the sand dunes
shifting overnight in a blast of wind
that can move mountains change the shape of worlds
in a grain of sand

this poet is mumbling
hoping that out of mumble might come lost words
lost places lost ways
sitting on a carved beach the wind in her face
the ocean flat as a mirror reflecting sky
trailing wisps of cloud

behind her is a world
unwanted unsettled unminded
and she too is un
undone unmade unravelled in the sun
that glare that unrelenting stare

what Queenie says about Altamira

you can tell by the shape of our bodies
we were a happy lot back then
the red ochre of our hides
the flaring of our horns

an ear in the earth
our likenesses
beginning
on ceilings near
the cave's mouth
continuing through
the multiple stomachs
of the cave's length

hands and hooves
like dance partners
under the gaze
of the nine-year-old girl
who found us
thousands of years later
her eyes not yet fogged
by disbelief

Queenie's aubade

morning's fingers prod you awake in the torrid zone
the day is off and running before you're really awake
cockatoos have finished their dawning screech
and the throat clearing of the kookaburra
turns into the day's first joke while the scrub hens
bicker even before dawn has come within

who cares where the sun beats when corals
grow into light who cares if the lace monitor
has found the eggs buried in the compost
or whether the waves are smashing at shore's edge
the hills creaking against the rising wind
all of it all of it is part of the day's beginning din

what really matters is that everything is packed
the time for doing and speaking all the things undone
and unspoken is gone the grass is rumpled earth pillows
damp with sorrow as we whisper into the dawning light
night is not half long enough when parting its undoing
our nostrils are wrapped between air and skin

string three

what the lovers say

on the horizon stand two cows at each step the earth
stretches out behind them trees and grasses grow
their horns are moons the lovers speak

1

how to contain
these feelings
only poems are
strong enough

2

they circle two blindfolded cows grinding mustard seed lost in
a haze of dust a world of eternal circles the daily grind how could
love change that?

we walk
separated by our untouching flanks

3

one day everything changes she nuzzles up close the smell of
mustard dust gone instead the smell of white fluid

we meet
lip to lip
sharing tongues
telltale bodies

4

morning is the time for flowers opening silently petals
spreading showing it need only happen once and the
whole world changes the world flips lips touch we hear
the recitation of akam

akam: Tamil: interior,
heart poems.

on a morning
bright with desire
the kurinci flowers

5

what was it her lover said? is that her on the corner of
the street nibbling petals and vegetable leaf?

what is this ache
huddling
between my ribs?
is it love?

6

she squanders time exchanges the possibility of hours
for a few minutes eyes meet through salt wet smiles

on a long afternoon
you look at me
and torrents wash me away

7

nights lengthen into light sleep untouched midnight grazing she
yawns her eyes wide open clouds pass birds call up dawn

my heart
is twisting and turning
like a restless sleeper

8

stone lies across her upper body cuneiform carved with a heavy
chisel the language of lust

I carry you around
your sound
etched on my heart

9

with the setting sun comes the scent of evening primrose yellow petals
frame her want a sickle moon carves a hollow space of memory she
sits on the ground looking up at the clear star-studded sky

on an evening
wretched with wanting
I remember
oh yes I remember

10

at night they walk on a beach an angel perches on the wall above
luminous green trees wave their arms against dark sky she flicks her
tail moves close she watches her companion

on a night
when no moon shines
your face is radiant

11

she listens to the chanting frogs the click rattles through her lifting
her spirits then hurling her down again tucks her legs tight
underneath above the sun shines in a cobalt sky

here you are again
nuzzling
the corners of my heart

12

on the street nine buffalo cows stroll by they lift their heads to
the sky calling rain piercing the clouds with their curved horns

dusk comes slowly
settles
evening clouds
rusted red

13

days are never-ending hollow tunnels

will it be one day
or three?
an eternity of moments
to wait through

14

from starvation to gluttony her mind runs in circles

my tongue
feasts on you

15

sounds fade and recede into a place behind hearing they wait at the
back of the tongue drones in waves from spine's end vibrating
through the body like a passion her call rumbles aa-um with
vibrato

we call through the night air
multilingual
fragments

16

dreams inhabit weird places clouds fly at the speed of sound the
morning's messenger is blushed pink sunrise clouds sweep
everything away washed clean and wretched again

oh to see your muzzle
by the pale light
of dawn

daybreak's pink strands
infiltrate your body

17

she mouths inarticulate sound oh ho ha she thinks seeing the other
move toward her

my aching heart
would like the taste
of salt lick again

18

drowsy days on the riverbank are easy they wander off
marking the earth with red hoof sutras

we walk
unseparated by our touching flanks

sūtra: Sanskrit: a line,
thread, string; a literary
form.

19

ancient feelings creep upon them the mysteries of the
moon the shape of cows' horns the scent of lilies the
memory of forget-me-nots the sweet cerise of sweet peas

did you know
that Ushas brings dawn
and her tongue is pink-tipped?

20

she seeks new experiences her mouth opens and she
swallows the world whole like a giant clam seagrass
swaying in the current new sounds in her ears the taste
of love on her tongue purple red leaves falling

oh the feel of you on my tongue

21

she inscribes memory just as hooves inscribe earth loose
as leaves bound tight as a show-cow's tail

my nose against yours
two bodies
sleeping

22

storms come and go they rise in the morning and slide away mid-afternoon hearts race out to greet weeping rain loss creeps in

was that your heart
I heard?

23

she tucks herself as tight as she can

I wrap you round me
like a cloak
of leaves

24

she looks down the throat of her lover there inside the mouth galactic swirl

the barest touch
a cheek lightly brushed

Queenie's loves

what Queenie says about the fugue of history

she runs for her life the music following
haunting every waking moment the voices
of those others weaving the gaps
like the woof and warp of a song

a song half forgotten half remembered
her life has turned contrapuntal
amnesic episodic amnesic again
days lost in fog clouds hanging over her head

wrapping it round swathed in a cloth of sound
she has always been the minor relative
never the major nor the dominant
black sheep can be a tonic but her story

her exposition is always chased away
for the refugee there is no chord
to hang her world on it is disappeared
like the girl with a fugue of memory

her identity lost her subject dissociated
a kind of shame no one will quite grasp
it is social death clearly warped she will not
attend the event after all no final entry

instead she is the eternal counterpoint
whose coda is a single
jubilant
voice

what she says about nomadic life

there are two ways of walking in the world
you can walk along a path in which your
colourful garments are a rainbow
or you can walk with your limbs
strung with ropes and string so you
resemble the downward pointing roots
of banyan trees in motion an ocean
of sound such as arises when a great herd
of cattle sways along a dusty road

what she says about wolves

slavering mouths are manifestations
of wolves of infinite appetites
taste and mutual lust
wolves in the night wood
flesh of betrayers
loyalty among wolves is not unknown
vegetarians are winning this one
on message against flesh

Artemis of the wild beasts
and ancient forests
settled ones arrive cut down forests
demonise their inhabitants
like the ancient herders
forever looking for the ideal pasture
terrified of the wolfish world

no whisperers among them
confusing bovine and wolverine
faces merging
calf and wolf as one
brown calf face outlined in forest black
fear rising like the hot season's temperature
time out of control
constant dread turning through the mind
the unknown the unknown the unknown

bovine: late Latin
bovinus, bovine f.:
belonging to the ox
tribe.

what the observer says about wolves

tails of wolves are bound
like sheaves of wheat
punishment for hunting down
domesticated ones

clouds shuffle across the sky
indigo and rainheavy
the snout of a loping wolf leads
clouds its tail trailing

a banyan tree is skyscraping
branches hunched like
sagging shoulders its fingers
scrape the ground

women slap the rumps of cows
who flick their tails at flies
deep inside the forest are
bright-coloured flowers

what she says about the gopī

their faces painted
smeared with white and yellow ochre
their lips blow air across leaves
making music at dawn while the sun
rolls into the morning sky
peacocks prance like dancing girls

at their feet the three-headed snake
slithers into the undergrowth
they lark about laughing at trifles
play on cloudswings made of rope
at evening after their day's frolicking
collapse into sleep on a feather bed

what Duhitri says

the youngest in the family
I milk the cows each day
the cow has many names
they call her gau and dhenu
they speak of duh it's what I do
squeeze milk from her dugs
in the doing of duh
I yield she yields
we give in every time

they call me
Duhitri
I am the milker
who draws down milk
I yearn for country
filled with duchas say the Irish
of their daughters
I am the yielder
they all take advantage of me
I am tochter dukte tu-ka-te
thugater *dhugheter daughter

duh: Sanskrit: to milk,
to yield.
dugs: dugdha
participle of duh:
milked.

duhitr: Sanskrit:
daughter, related to
the word for milker.

dúchas: Irish: a feeling
for country or heritage.

what Radha says to Mura

I live in three worlds amphibious as I am
my tongue is dextrous she the sakhī
is my companion of the night
forest companion love companion

sakhī: Sanskrit:
female friend or
lover.

we bathe in the river leaving our skins
on shore feel the flush of fluid
against our thighs the warmth surrounding us
we swim daily against the current

some days I wander forest paths
creeping into all the secret clefts
it's a florid wilderness the leaves
of vines quiver like love in a fever

when the bees appear they dance
and I dance with them from hive
to flower and back again we all dance
my companions and I just like the bees

some days I've been racked by the poison
of love my body cruelly pained with feeling
reeling with moodiness sleepless sweaty
nights when even the moon tosses and turns

when the cranes fly in we all go a bit mad
with the season's heat their wings make
an alphabet against the indigo cloud
darkness descends early with moisture

Mura sings to me old songs she knows them all
like some strange magic her voice soothes me
caresses me her silken words voluptuous
accompanied by the jangle of bangles

Mura: a gopī and
friend of Rādhā,
also a gopī.

125

it's Mura who loves me most and I too her
but I cannot be her everything she's as light
as feathered hibiscus my night-lily petals
weigh me down with sudden passions

Mura sing to me again let me hear the sound
of your flute the beat of your tambourine
let me hear the tap of your hooves
as you dance on this flat rock this spinning ground

what Mura says to Radha

I'm the singer in the group my song
follows Radha follows as she walks
the forest paths she revels in her body
udder swaying to the dance of bees

she's playful almost drunk with dancing
protected by the ornaments she wears
on her legs I sing the rainbow of her body
light fractured shining through skin's prism

we are gopi girls our bellies are snake pits
muscles writhe and flex throb and dance
our days are by turns languid and dynamic
it's not enchantment simply friendship

the language of the goddess is on my lips
as each day I tend her with song my words
hers I can't say I'm always fair some days
my lips are scorched with jealousy

as she pays attention to this gopi or that
the seamstress the fruit picker the bread maker
the veena player we all want her gaze
I walk away flick my tail like a tiger

what Queenie says to the gopī

so it's a secret gopi girls?
you who hide among the cows
who caress their quivering flanks
in secret places where only you
do not fear to go

do you too cover your face in
clay white as the milky way?
you weave light as it bends
curves along an infinite edge
kissing eternity's face

when the gopi lock eyes
stars meld collapse in a moment
of singularity don't mess with
these girls their curls
are like steel

sent to protect the cow at the
centre of the universe gift giver
vivifier they dance to their own tune
it's a sham this flute-playing
androgyne

this boy who dances and flirts
he has no interest in skirts or skirls
Suniti got it right and Gertrude too
the cow leapt the moon for you and me
for me and for you

what her lover says about raga

in spring the gopi dance
the vasant raga
trees bow to them
flowers blossom in full regalia

rāga: Sanskrit: colour,
hue; passion; musical
note, harmony, melody.
vasant: spring; season
of love.

they dance at night
under moon and stars
their throats strumming
their lips humming

Radha dressed in reds
and greens flings her arms

129

what she sings to her maiden aunt

you who flank me
whose inheritance is never direct but diagonal
I read your lips slant my maiden aunt

you who groom me with stories of youth
of rebellion and wild love
I read your body slant my maiden aunt

you who sing whistle and dance
your flamboyant style is profound
I read your hands slant my maiden aunt

you who find me in far places
dreams of travel achieved
I read your feet slant my maiden aunt

you who heard my wish
smiled said yes and more
I read your fingers slant my maiden aunt

you who embraced me
never felt disgrace
I read your heart slant my maiden aunt

what sixty-four dakinis say in one voice

they call me demon
it's obvious I never do
the expected at the time
it is expected
instead I hover like a bird
wings fluttering and shivering
stroking the moon

I carry a cup of blood
my blood and her blood
I refuse to braid my hair
I run across the night sky
my hair trailing
my knife curving
like the moon

I stand in eight figures
of eight a forcefield
holding the petals closed
the moon is held low
I drink sky dew
open the petals
reveal the flower's heart

they shiver with fear
no spine any of them
scared of their honour
they say *she's demonic*
you should see her
with a broom
witch witch

what we sing in one voice

eine Frau: German:
a woman, one woman.

go out to the world of cow
the names we're called are knives
sing sing into night for we are eine Frau
call out for us do not betray us now
your day's good your time finite
go out to the world of cow
the sky is wild nightbirds call winds sough
behind the moonrise shifting tides
sing sing into night for we are eine Frau
we sit together on the bough
we women who walk at night
go out to the world of cow
exiled in Moscow Kracow and Macau
we've paid too much now in tithes
sing sing into night for we are eine Frau
the boats are leaving she is at the prow
her gnat-maddened skin a bloom of hives
go out to the world of cow
sing sing into night for we are eine Frau

what she says about akam

the ancient Tamil poet
writes of love
what she says
what her girlfriend says
the message is passed
along the line

and so I will write
of the red-beaked
black swan
here on this lagoon
in its thousands
hooting
like a crowd
of women with
only their eyes showing

they call it akam
inscapes
heart poems
hearth poems
where a woman's love
is the sudden
kurinci bloom

I ask *is it as short-lived*
as the one-day flower?

kōlam: Tamil:
ornamental lines or
figures drawn on the
floor.

what she says about kolam

where they are drawn and when
is all important

early morning is auspicious
it sets the shape of the day

the hard ground is
cleaned
points of white grain sprinkled

she works quickly
she knows her design for the day
runs the powdered grain
from point to point

it is a mandala
a yantra
a sign

yantra: Sanskrit:
instrument for
restraining; fetter, rein;
mystical diagram.

so the forces of the universe
align themselves

with her intentions

what she says about dancers

the dancers' names are engraved in red stone
ancient as our dreams ancient as this language

of flowers seasons landscapes and mood
the woman dances and her girlfriend
asks who she is pining for?
why she is in a cow sulk?
the girlfriend dances
gives her the marutam
the queen's flower
while the woman's mother
tells her old stories of passion and heat
monsoon and desire and tears

the dancers' names are engraved in stone
ancient as our dreams ancient like this language

what she says about the shore temple

at the temple a herd of cows
waiting for the sea to stop
its ceaseless waves
these cows sit stone-faced
crows leap from rump
to rump and back again
the sea flows on
wave after wave

cow faces worn down
by seaspray smoothed
the angles no longer sharp
the temple eroded
sand salt and water
these cows sit and wait
as eternity passes by
in the feathers of a crow

what Queenie says about the word paksha

pakṣa: Sanskrit:
the shape of the
waning moon; a wing.

moon wing floats overhead in the dark
of the lunar month
fish fin swims by beneath
the water's edge
cow flank is a night feather against my shoulder
smelling of chaff and straw
party factions are armies' phalanxes
still smoking in noisy backrooms
every proposition is an equation to be argued
by show-off peacocks spreading feathers
her hands articulate like wingbones
when she dances an elephant will dance
and cry when the moon's wings
are clipped

what Anaktoria says to Sappho

when the herds are running the ground thrumming
sunlight scaling every beam of dust like a horde
on the move your finest poems are for me
that's what I love best

when the sun strikes your coat roàn with heat
we all stand dazzled by your beauty
and none of us will ever abandon you
you the brightest of us all

when the summer grass grows pale
and the longing strikes up again
I think of you standing always knowing
which way to go

your doubts are few your face dewy
in the morning light and your eyes
brown soft but your glance is as sharp
as thorns

let me follow you on this track
into that thicket by the river
let us stand flank by flank
our love our armour

what she says about Atthis

Atthis is in the temple
they have painted her limbs
her forehead is floral

she likes this temple
on a hilltop where she watches
as dawn scrambles into day

at dusk she faces the other direction
when day lowers itself into night
this is the best season

the grass is lush
buttercups are plentiful
the air cool and clear

since she became a temple cow
life has been easier
each day sixteen girls

clamour around her in the meadow
fuss over her
stroke and brush her flanks

but she misses her friend
the ever-shrewd and delightful
milky-faced Sappho

who thrived in the herd
she loved to lead
lowing her tunes

and soon the young heifers
are prancing behind
moaning and shaking their heads in time

rubbing tree branches as they tread
but she is gone
these girls are her music now

what the others say about Sappho

a gap a space a hole a lacuna
she is a fragment a figment
a crack a fissure a perforation
she is a blank page an oblivion
a tear a breach a slit a pause
she is empty a void shunya
an egret perches on the spine of the cow

what Gongyla says

when winter ices my coat
when it strikes
the heart
whatever can you do

she has made it public
her longing for me
she wants me to sing
my heart pain

she says Aphrodite
is hard-hearted
her love searing
but all I want

is want

what Sappho says about Andromeda

the tip of your nose
is as pink as your morning tongue
your spiral tail visible at night
as you approach our island in space

once they said we were rivals
but I'm a city creature
and you a farm girl
where's the rivalry in that?

what she says about sedentary life

the cattle yard
is a surprising place
a place where so much goes on

these gopi have made
camp here by the river
every day the eldest rises early

bucolic: Latin:
bucolicus;
βουκολικη: Greek:
of or pertaining to
herdswomen.

in bucolic calm
raises hands to the sky
plucking the sun from its sleep

red cows chorus the morning
with their sacred droning
Rohini's flanks are smeared

with flowing milk
her thighs shine in a mystery
of oceanic light

what Madhukarī says

madhukarī: Sanskrit: honey-maker, bee.

has the bee stung your lip?
where love stings there lies the hurt

let the dance take me in its swarm
rise like the sun in spring
the vines embrace me
flowers nod a jig in the breeze

on your body lines of ash
like the pattern of the dance
a dalliance of girls swaying

somewhere beneath the horizon
come the sounds of a raga
each pada of the song
in the rhythm of the herd
hear the beat of the hooves

pāda: Sanskrit: foot of person or animal; a poetic foot.

the dancers approach
a cloud of bodies
raising gusts of wind
cow dust is on your coat
cow dust is in my breath

I am the rasa
I am the lover in the dance
my footsteps in yours
touching like wind breath

rasa: Sanskrit: juice of plants; melted butter; nectar; body fluid; taste; sentiment, desire.

the dancer bristles
grass trembles
on the river's edge

what Radha says

I gave my love not for wealth
not for social standing
not for security or stability
but because I must

you came to me
and I to you
like flames burning
fragile
as candle breath
dangerous
as wildfire

I gave my love
in spite of fragility
and danger

I lost my family
friends left in droves
some refused
to speak with me
turned their backs
razed me with their eyes

I gave my love
because nothing else
in the world matters
more

what the Indian heifer says about priya

priya: Sanskrit:
a term of endearment.

soft on the mouth this word for beloved
as soft as parrot feathers
the look of a friend

the heifer runs not with garlands
she runs to catch the goose taking off
heading south for summer

the food here is expensive
and vultures pay more
for fresh fallen mangoes

priya describes the way a cow
will nuzzle up to another
muzzling tongues wandering

what Queenie says about love

I sing the thrilling body take it to pinnacles
and profundities heave over precipices
flex its muscled being and quivering mouth
it's some kind of operatic acrobat peddling
her wares on busker street singing aching arias
her tongue a glacier sliding across the world

I think the rousing mind its metaphysics
a constant convocation of thoughts moulding
the world a cosmos of rhinoceros beetles hissing
frogs barking birds chasing on bulky legs
the orbit of life around her more exciting
than all the ponderous tomes of lore

what Queenie says about inversion

when I amble outside tonight the wind is at my feet the two
half moons are my eyes I am nothing special just a cow who
wants to change the world a cow whose eyes are on the sky

when I walk the city streets my head is in the gutter all I can see
are the black shoelaces of men in suits who walk past me with
heads in the air not seeing a thing at their feet

when I go to the mall the skylights are beneath me they are
mind puzzles with udder clouds they float in patterns above the
stocktaking sales the zing of the new machines gobbling cards

when I run the beach on my head I am the complete
beachcomber my head in the sand the sand on my head coral
skulls lie about and the dogs run with them in their mouths

what she sings to her sister

oh sister stay / stay with me sister
might we be as sisters
reside with me inside my skin

oh sister stay / stay with me sister
let us be sisters in friendship
reside with me inside my skin

oh sister stay / stay with me sister
let my want be your want
reside with me inside my skin

oh sister stay / stay with me sister
may your hand be held in mine
reside with me inside my skin

oh sister stay / stay with me sister
may we vibrate like strings in harmony
reside with me inside my skin

string four

what Queenie says about the philosophy cow

> If ultimately we are denied a new social order, which
> therefore can exist only in words, I will find it in myself.
>
> Monique Wittig
> *The Straight Mind*

human or bovine
land cow or sea cow
we stand on a precipice

Sappho's cliff was poetic
it was high
nothing to do but fly
thrill at the drop
disappear and always
be remembered

that's the heard story
what really happened?
did she get old
pull out the slippers and shawl
as winter curled around her shoulders?
tell stories and sing songs
to her companion lovers?

perhaps there's an altogether
different story
a story about
taking off in a small boat
to see the world

she didn't go alone
but with companionship
a whispered story
about a group of women
landing on the shores of Asia Minor
gateway to the rest of Asia
Asia Major

they strolled into the local market
looked at the horses
all knew how to choose a good horse
so the tales went
and though not short on cash
the sellers didn't seem able to keep their prices up
they stayed a few days in this shore town
purchased provisions blankets shawls
the odd small memento
they did not buy jewellery or kohl or perfume
and the stallholders became angry
all sorts of stories circulated after they left
but who knows which are true

some tell that the group rode
right to where the sun rises
at the edge of the world

others say they died
of a mysterious disease

yet others say they rode
until they found a deserted valley
set up camp settled down
and to this day remain hidden
in a valley where no man dares

they raise cows goats and sheep
but do not eat meat

they make fine fabrics
their dyes deep and true
their carpets among the best you can find
the only way to buy these
is for the women to go
select their favourites
and return with a strange
kind of silence about them
they never speak
of what they have seen
occasionally one does not return

questions are raised
about how they have continued
but it's easy
you walk over the mountain
disguised as a local
from a town far enough away
to pass as one of the people unknown
men do not look closely
when sex is offered lightly
keep it random
and it's easily maintained

but these are fables
we all know

that such a story
cannot be true

is it any less believable
than tales of dragons
or wars
        or magic
                or love?

who says that we should be
the only people on earth
without stories?

what Queenie sings to us

chaos is all the rage as the world warms
and the tropics move north and south
winds build and once again the fish gods
try to come ashore *halleluiah alleluia* they cry

it's the cow who wins the prize for the
broadest back whether she be whale or
elephant or one of the domestic kind she
is always big *halleluiah alleluia* they cry

the earth is but a speck of dust in this whirl
our galaxy from some angles resembles
the crescent moon from others
the shape of a horn *halleluiah alleluia* they cry

the night lotus opens blue as sky you are draped
in a shawl a dupatta the colour of evening
the cushion on which you are sitting is
a golden bee *halleluiah alleluia* they cry

blood courses from our bodies but we are not
warriors existence is vital we are never
at ease each has encountered her own
private pain *halleluiah alleluia* they cry

the rain clouds are returning and your body
shines in the water-filled light you might have
ploughed fields tracing out the boustrophedon
with your hooves *halleluiah alleluia* they cry

instead you have become one of those fist-raisers
a troublemaker in the bleachers you write poems
thrilling to a music that lifts you daily celebrating
unbelievable truths *halleluiah alleluia* they cry

notes

a note on pronunciation

Indian languages have several s sounds. Unadorned s sounds like s in serious; ṣ (with dot underneath) is a retroflex s which, to English ears, sounds like sh; ś (with accent over s) also sounds like sh.

In Sanskrit th sounds like th in hothead.

All letters with dots underneath are retroflex. If you put your tongue on the roof of your mouth behind your teeth, you'll come close to making the right sound.

Long vowels – those with diacritics over them – are lengthened, so the first syllable in Rāvana is long while the others are short. In English we tend to lengthen the second syllable.

notes on poems

PAGE 4

Al-Lat: Pre-Islamic Arabian goddess. Along with her sisters Manāt and Al-'Uzzá, Al-Lat was one of the three chief goddesses of Mecca.

Latona: Latin name of Greek Leto (mother of the twins, Artemis and Apollo); her Latin name is influenced by Etruscan Letun.

Leda: her name may be related to Lycian Leto. She is the mother of Helen and Klytemnestra and of Kastor and Pollux (also known as the Dioskouri).

PAGE 12

Meena: Sanskrit for fish; daughter of Uṣas, Vedic goddess of dawn. In Greek, the word for cow ἡ βοῦς is also a word for fish, in particular a fish of the Nile. In Latin, bos, bovis has as its second meaning 'a kind of flat fish'.

This poem is based on a story told to V. Geetha by her South Indian Muslim friend (of another name), in turn told to me. The story is used with permission from both storytellers.

boson: named after Indian mathematician Satyendra Nath Bose (1894–1974), a boson is a subatomic force carrier particle in quantum physics. Bosons with the same energy can inhabit the same place in space (like and like do not repel). Elementary bosons are also called photons, W and Z particles, and gluons.

Sītā: a foundling, regarded as a daughter of Bhudevi, the earth goddess. Her name means furrow, the line of a ploughshare; she was discovered in a furrow of a ploughed field. A principal character in the epic Rāmāyaṇa and married to Rāma.

Rāvaṇa: the demon king of Laṅkā.

Rāma the exiled king of Ayodhya.

Written after watching *Sita Sings the Blues*, an animated movie by Nina Paley.

Cleis: daughter of Sappho.

Demeter: Greek goddess of cereal crops. Although in later mythology she is Persephone's mother, it's likely that earlier renditions of the myth included Demeter (mother), Kore (young woman), Persephone (queen of the underworld).

Persephone: abducted by Hades, god of the underworld. Persephone is doomed to remain in the underworld for the winter months because she ate the pomegranate offered to her. When she is released in spring, her mother, Demeter, celebrates the return of her daughter with good crop harvests.

Ekaterina: Hecate: Greek goddess of the underworld (possibly identical to Persephone), sometimes represented with three bodies; sister to the sun god, Helios.

Baubo: in the *Homeric Hymn to Demeter*, Baubo makes Demeter laugh by telling ribald jokes or showing her genitals.

Trivia: Roman goddess equivalent to Greek Hekate, goddess associated with three-way crossroads and the moon.

Hektor: Trojan prince and son of Priam and Hekuba whose brother Paris elopes with Helen, the queen of Sparta and sister of Klytemnesta (mother of Elektra). Hektor is killed by Achilles on the battlefield. Instead of immediately returning Hektor's body to the city of Troy for proper mourning rituals, Achilles drags the body of Hektor around the walls of Troy.

kuvalaya: a water-lily, especially the blue water-lily that opens at night. It can also mean lotus-eyed or a handsome woman.

Sārasvatī: Indian goddess of writing, knowledge and music.

Deepavali or Diwali: a five-day festival of lights celebrated by Hindus, Sikhs and Jains between mid-October and mid-November. In Hinduism it is connected to the battle between Rāma and Rāvana over Sītā.

Elektra: daughter of Klytemnestra and Agamemnon, sister of Orestes, Iphigeneia and Chrysothemis. All are mythic figures in the *Iliad* and the *Odyssey*.

Lakṣmī: Indian goddess of wealth and good fortune.

Ereshkigal: Sumerian goddess of the underworld, sister of Inanna, queen of heaven (Inanna is sometimes known as Ishtar).

Io: priestess of Hera who was disguised as a heifer.

Hera: Pre-Homeric Greek goddess whose roots in the archaic period of Greek history (800–480 BCE) suggest that she is identical to the Great Goddess of Minoan Crete. The cow and the peacock are sacred to her and a frequent epithet is 'cow-eyed'.

temenos: precinct of land dedicated to a deity.

PAGE 41

Hathor: Egyptian cow goddess; on her head is a sun disk enclosed by curved cow horns. She is also a sky goddess.

PAGE 42

Guinevere was a childless queen. In the Welsh tradition of the medieval period, Guinevere was abducted and held captive in a castle for a year. This story resembles the tale of Sītā's abduction in the *Rāmayāṇa*, as well as the abduction of Persephone.

PAGE 43

Durga: a very old and powerful ten-armed Indian goddess who rides a lion and carries a spear with which she kills the buffalo demon. Durga Puja is held each year around September. It is a major festival in Bangladesh, Nepal and the northeastern states of India.

PAGE 45

Kalypso: in Greek the word kalypso means covered or concealed. Odysseus is swept on to Kalypso's island where she keeps him hidden until ordered by the immortals to let him go.

PAGE 46

Sāvitṛ: a character in the epic *Mahābhārata* who outwits the god of death, Yama.

Simone Weil: French philosopher and member of the Resistance; she died at the age of thirty-four from tuberculosis and perhaps self-starvation.

Yama: god of death; in some traditions he has a twin sister Yamī.

PAGE 47

'105-yr-old virgin owes long life to no sex', *Daily Telegraph*, October 10, 2008.

PAGE 49

Mount Maṇḍara is mentioned in the Purāṇas and was used as an inverted top to churn the ocean of milk.

159

Saramā and the sun cow draws on a story from the *Ṛg Veda* (10/108/1–11). Saramā, the messenger dog, is sent off in search of the stolen cow.

Nicothoe, Aellopus, Ocypete, Harpys, Ocypus, Propontis, Echinades, Strophades: these names are listed in Hesiod's *Catalogue of Women*.

Iphigeneia: daughter of Agamemnon, sacrificed by him en route to Troy in order to raise the winds; according to other traditions she is rescued and lands in Tauris (modern-day Crimea) where she becomes a priestess in the temple of Artemis.

Diotima: Diotima of Mantinea, Greece was born around 470–450 BCE. In Plato's *Symposium*, Socrates credits her with his philosophical discourse on 'becoming' and the nature of the human soul. The *Symposium* was written around 385 BCE. Conventionally, philosophers have argued that she is a fictitious character, while simultaneously maintaining that all the men are real.

Gargi Vachaknavi is a renowned Indian philosopher who is mentioned in the *Bṛihadāraṇyaka*, one of the earliest *Upaniṣads* written between 1000 and 300 BCE. It is likely Gargi lived in India around 600 BCE.

Yajnavalka: ancient Indian sage. In one tradition he claims the prize of a thousand cows even before the competition begins. He is said to have won the competition as the greatest sage of his time. Gargi challenged Yajnavalka on the nature of the soul.

Tocharian: ancient Indo-European language of Central Asia; although no longer spoken, it is an important language in comparative linguistics.

Gandhari: ancient spoken language of the northwestern area of the Indian subcontinent.

Prākrit: probably older than Sanskrit, the language used in the street rather than in religious discourse; Prākrit is the language "actually spoken" (Doniger 2009).

Sanskrit: ancient Indian language used in religious ritual; mostly spoken by men.

Tamil: Dravidian language spoken by people of South India; Sangam literature dates from 100 BCE to 250 CE.

Pali: a Prākrit language of India and the language of many early Buddhist scriptures.

PAGE 84

sandhi: Sanskrit: joining; refers to changes in the spelling of words according to the effect neighbouring letters have on the sounds produced.

Rohini: a red cow; a cow of plenty; Rohini is the Indian name for Aldebaran, the brightest star in the constellation of Taurus.

PAGE 87

subhāṣita: a good or eloquent speech, comparable to a proverb or saying in English; subāshitāni are sung or chanted and are also used as language mnemonics.

poikilophrōn: many hued, multi-coloured mind; the first word in Sappho's hymn to Aphrodite; in some readings it is poikilothrōn which means many-coloured throne.

PAGE 89

gaur: *Bos gaurus*, previously *Bibos gauris*, the largest bovine species on earth, found in India.

PAGE 92

Uṣas: Indian goddess of dawn, carried in a chariot yoked to seven cows, seven rays.

PAGE 95

gopuram: literally cow town, an elaborate tower on South Indian temples.

PAGE 96

tulasi: Tamil: the herb basil, considered holy. The English word basil comes from the Greek word basileia: queen; basileus: of god or Zeus; related to basilica.

PAGE 102

Sarasvathi: South Indian spelling of Sarasvati, goddess of writing, knowledge and music.

PAGE 106

Altamira: an Upper Paleolithic cave in Spain with a herd of hooved animals painted

161

on the ceiling, including bison, horses, deer and goats. The nine-year-old unnamed daughter of amateur archaeologist Marcelino Sanz de Sautuola found the cave in 1879.

PAGE 110

akam: interior poems of the Tamil Sangam tradition, often about love. Interior refers to the heart, and the seven kinds of love are each associated with particular landscapes, flowers, birds, seasons, as well as water courses and people.

kuṟiñci: a flower from the Nilgiri Hills area in Tamil Nadu that blooms profusely once every twelve years (*Strobilanthes kunthiana*). In the Sangam tradition the kuṟiñci is associated with the lovers' union.

PAGE 121

Artemis: Greek goddess of the forests and wild beasts, she is an archer and is accompanied by dogs; sister of Apollo.

PAGE 124

There are many words for cow in Sanskrit, the two most commonly used are gau and dhenu.

dugs: pap or udder of female mammalian, also teat or nipple; as applied to a woman's breast, now contemptuous.

Indo-European languages possess many resemblances in the words for daughter. Here are some of them: Tochter: German; dukte: Lithuanian; tu-ka-te: Linear B Greek; *dhugeter: Proto-Indo-European; thugater: Greek: slave is an additional given meaning.

PAGE 125

Rādhā: leader of many cowherd girls or gopī from the village of Vrindāvan where the god, Kṛṣṇa, spent his childhood. The story is told in the *Mahābhārata*, the *Bhāgavata Purāṇa* and in the *Gīta Govinda*. In bhakti traditions Rādhā is considered the supreme goddess, the original Shakti.

PAGE 128

Suniti: Indian poet and fabulist, Suniti Namjoshi, author of *The Conversations of Cow*.

Gertrude: American writer, Gertrude Stein (1874–1946). She famously wrote:

'Alice had a cow'.

PAGE 129

rāga: a series of at least five notes upon which a melody is built. Rāgas are associated with different seasons and times of day. Indian classical music is always rāga-based.

PAGE 131

ḍākinī: a yogini, sky wanderer or dancer, sometimes regarded as a female embodiment of enlightened energy. Ḍākinīs have associations with the mātrikas and their sixty-four manifestations.

PAGE 132

her gnat-maddened skin a bloom of hives: a reference to the poem 'Monster' by Robin Morgan which I first encountered in the pirate edition of *Monster* (1973) published by Melbourne Radical Feminists. The lines read: May my hives bloom bravely until my flesh is aflame / and burns through the cobwebs. / May we go mad together, my sisters.

PAGE 134

kōlam: patterns drawn by women using rice flour at entrances to houses. The patterns are drawn at dawn.

PAGE 135

marutam: the queen's flower is important in akam poetry; it symbolises unfaithfulness and sulking scenes; also associated with buffalo.

PAGE 136

shore temple: a reference to the temple at Mahabalipuram (also known as Mamallapuram) in Tamil Nadu, India.

PAGE 137

pakṣa: Sanskrit words have a wide semantic arc. The main meanings of pakṣa are the shape of the waning moon, a wing; others are contained in this poem.

PAGE 138

Anaktoria: a companion of Sappho, whom Sappho mentions in her love poems.

Sappho: poet, born between 630 and 612 BCE on Lesbos off the coast of modern-day Turkey. Sappho died around 570 BCE. The inventor of lyric poetry and the myxolydian musical mode, she wrote poetry and songs in Aolian Greek. Her most recently discovered poem – about old age – was published in 2005.

PAGE 139

Atthis: said to be a lover of Sappho.

PAGE 142

Gongyla: one of Sappho's companions.

PAGE 143

Andromeda: a companion of Sappho; a spiral galaxy.

PAGE 155

boustrophedon: Greek: an ancient method of ploughing in which two cows retrace their steps in parallel lines; also a method of writing.

sources

Barnard, Mary (tr.). 1958. *Sappho: A new translation*. Berkeley: University of California Press.

Carson, Anne (tr.). 2003. *If Not, Winter: Fragments of Sappho*. New York: Vintage.

Deboy, Bibek. 2008. *Sarama and Her Children: The dog in Indian myth*. New Delhi: Penguin.

Doniger, Wendy. 2009. *The Hindus: An alternative history*. New Delhi: Penguin.

Fabricius, Johann Philipp. 1972. *J.P. Fabricius's Tamil and English Dictionary*. 4th ed., revised and enlarged. Tranquebar: Evangelical Lutheran Mission Publishing House.

Gubser, Steven S. 2010. *The Little Book of String Theory*. Princeton: Princeton University Press.

Hamburger, Michael (tr.). 2002. *Poems of Paul Celan*. New York: Persea Books.

Hammond, N.G.L and H.H. Scullard. 1979. *The Oxford Classical Dictionary*. Oxford: Oxford University Press.

Hawthorne, Susan. 1993. 'Diotima Speaks through the Body.' In *Engendering Origins: Critical feminist essays in Plato and Aristotle*, Bat-Ami Bar On (ed.). Albany: State University of New York Press.

Hesiod. 2008. *Catalogue of Women*. Hugh G. Evelyn-White (tr.). Gutenberg Project.

Hine, Daryl (tr.). 2005. *Works of Hesiod and the Homeric Hymns*. Chicago: University of Chicago Press.

Liddell, Henry George and Robert Scott. 1996. *A Greek-English Lexicon*. Oxford: Oxford University Press.

Monier-Williams, Monier. 2002. *A Sanskrit-English Dictionary*. Delhi: Motilal Banarsidass Publishers.

Morgan, Robin. 1973. *Monster*. Melbourne: Melbourne Radical Feminists.

Namjoshi, Suniti. 1985. *Conversations with Cow*. London: The Women's Press.

Page, Denys L. 1986. *Lyrica Graeca Selecta*. Oxford: Oxford University Press.

Ruden, Sarah (tr.). 2005. *Homeric Hymns*. Indianapolis: Hackett Publishing Company.

Salma. 2009. *The Hour Past Midnight*. Lakshmi Holmstrom (tr.). New Delhi: Zubaan.

Shorter Oxford English Dictionary on Historical Principles. 1977. Oxford: Oxford University Press.

Spraggs, Gillian. 2006. Sappho: Fragment 58 (a). http://www.gillianspraggs.com/translations/sappho58a.html

Stein, Gertrude. 1926. *A Book Concluding with As a Wife Has a Cow, A Love Story*. Paris: Editions de la Galerie Simon.

Stein, Gertrude. 1989. *Lifting Belly*. Tallahassee: The Naiad Press.

Thadani, Giti. 1996. *Sakhiyani: Lesbian desire in ancient and modern India*. London: Cassells.

Thangappa, M.L. (tr.). 2010. *Love Stands Alone: Selections from Tamil Sangam poetry*. New Delhi: Viking.

Walker, Barbara. 1983. *The Woman's Encyclopedia of Myths and Secrets*. San Francisco: Harper & Row.

West, Martin L. 2005. A New Sappho Poem. *Times Literary Supplement 5334*, June 24: p. 8.

Wittgenstein, Ludwig. 1974. *Tractatus Logico-Philosophicus*. Pears, David and Brian McGuiness (trs.). London: Routledge & Kegan Paul.

Wittig, Monique. 1992. *The Straight Mind and Other Essays*. Boston: Beacon Press.